THE
GOLFER'S
BOOK *of* DAYS

**Facts, Feats and Folklore
from the World of Golf**

PERCY HUGGINS

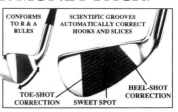

THE GOLFER'S BOOK OF DAYS

Percy Huggins

First published in the United Kingdom by The Edinburgh Publishing
Company Limited, Whittingehame, East Lothian, Scotland.

British Library Cataloguing in Publication Data

Huggins, Percy

Golfer's Book of Days, 1993

I. Title

796.352

ISBN 1 874201 04 8

*Cover illustration: The Fifth Tee, St. Andrews, 1921 by John Sutton by
kind permission of the Eaton Gallery, London and The Bridgeman
Art Library, London.*

Printed and bound in the United Kingdom by
Stephens & George Ltd, Merthyr Industrial Estate, Dowlais, Merthyr Tydfil, Mid Glamorgan, CF48 2TD

CONTENTS

THE HOT IRON GOT HOTTER

Tommy Armour

3

PAT. PEND.

CAVITY BALANCED

845s

SILVER SCOT

The switch to the Silver Scot® 845s® irons continues to grow. And the latest surveys* confirm it.

And for good reason: they play as good as they look. They give the better player everything he wants, and the average player everything he needs.

More serious golfers are switching to 845s irons. More average players, single digit handicappers and PGA Tour pros like Christy O'Connor Jnr., Andrew Murray and Adam Hunter are choosing the 845s irons.

Also available for lefties and women, 845s irons feature Golf Pride® Victory Grips and your choice of steel shafts by True Temper® or our high performance G-Force® Graphite shafts.

Out there, somewhere, there may be a limit to how hot an iron can get. We just haven't found it yet. Try an 845s iron, and find out why.

Tommy Armour
GOLF

Tommy Armour Golf (Scotland) Ltd, 2 Lindsay Square, Deans Southwest Industrial Estate, Livingston EH54 8LG, West Lothian, Scotland.
Telephone: (0506) 417858. Fax: (0506) 417773

*1991 Darrell Consumer Survey
1991 Sports Guide Golf Census

INTRODUCTION

Back in 1955 I found myself, on the outskirts of Chicago, on a golf course that had a telephone extension on every tee. The idea, apparently was that members, in the course of a round, could keep in touch with their offices, to discover what was happening on the stock market. The course, I understand, has long vanished from the horizon as the builders have moved in - and I am not surprised. One of the attractions of golf, for the ordinary club member, and for those who play on public courses, is that it enables them to get away from it all. Whether you are playing well or badly you have to be so engrossed with what you are doing, or how your score is going, or how the match is progressing, that there is simply no room for any other thoughts. It has been said that it never rains on the golf course, and there is much truth in that. Many years ago, in a classic final in the British Ladies Championship, one of the contenders holed a vital putt on the 11th green at Troon (now Royal Troon) as a train thundered past, only yards away. Later, when she eventually emerged triumphant at the 37th hole, she was asked if she had not been distracted by the passing train. Puzzled, she responded, "What train?".

For me, golf has been a fascination, in all its aspects, for more than half a century, ever since I attended my first Open Championship in a journalistic capacity in 1936.

During the last two decades, or more, I have been frequently asked, usually by other golf enthusiasts who have listened most flatteringly to some of my anecdotes and memories, why I have never written a book. The simple answer is that I never found the time. Then, in retirement, I was approached by the publishers planning *The Golfer's Book of Days*, to produce editorial content for it. While I shall never know I suspect that the publishers were guided in my direction by someone who had once said to me "Why don't you write a book?" I accepted the invitation.

It has given me the opportunity to put in print anecdotes that many had found of interest, recollections of happenings during my close-to-six-decades of involvement in the game, and stories told to me by colleagues who were veterans when I was young and who could go back in memory to the days of the famous Triumvirate. I trust the users of *The Golfer's Book of Days* will find the facts, figures and anecdotes it contains will give them as much reading pleasure as the writing of them has given me pleasure.

Percy Huggins
Clarkston, nr. Glasgow, Scotland

RECORD ACHIEVEMENTS IN GOLF

There have been many outstanding golfing records over the years. The following are some of the most interesting:

In 1930 an amateur from Atlanta, Georgia, R.T. (Bobby) Jones, achieved what became known as the "Grand Slam" when he won both the open and the amateur championships in Britain and the United States that year. He then retired from competitive golf at the age of 28. By then he had won the Open Championship three times, the U.S. Championship four times (in additional to losing two play-offs for the title) and the U.S. Amateur Championship five times. His only victory in the Amateur Championship (sometimes described nowadays, but incorrectly, as the British Amateur Championship) was in 1930.

It is highly unlikely that Jones's achievement will ever be equalled and it is now felt that the modern day equivalent would be a victory for a professional in each of the U.S. Masters, the U.S. Open Championship, the Open Championship and the U.S.P.G.A. Championship in one year. To date no one has achieved that feat and Ben Hogan is the only player to have won three of those four events in a single season. He did so in 1953, when he won the Masters, the U.S. Open and the Open (the only time he competed in the event). He could not bid for the 1953 U.S.P.G.A. Championship as well because, that year, it overlapped the Open Championship.

Four players have won the Open Championship with their score in each round lower than in the previous one. The first to do so was Jack White, at Royal St. George's, Sandwich in 1904 with rounds of 80, 75, 72 and 69. Two years later James Braid won at Muirfield with rounds of 77, 76, 74 and 73. In 1953, in his only appearance in the event, Ben Hogan (U.S.) won with rounds of 73, 71, 70 and 68. Six years later Gary Player (South Africa) won at Muirfield with 75, 71, 70 and 68.

An aggregate of 132 scored by Henry Cotton for the first two rounds of the Open Championship at Royal St.George's, Sandwich in 1934 (67-65) has never been bettered though it had twice been equalled (in 1990) until Nick Faldo established a new record of 130 in the 1992 championship (66-64). - see page 126.

When Fred Bullock (Royal Lytham and St. Annes) tied for the seventh place in the 1950 Open Championship at Troon (now Royal Troon) he did so with four rounds of 71, for an aggregate of 284.

OLD AND YOUNG TOM MORRIS
- BOTH FATHER AND SON
WON THE OPEN 4 TIMES

Tom Morris Junior became the youngest ever winner of the Open Championship, when he captured the title for the first time in 1868, when 17 years of age, and just some 20-odd days short of being $17\frac{1}{2}$.

Tom Morris, sometimes known as Old Tom Morris to distinguish him from his son Young Tom Morris, is the oldest winner of the Open Championship at the age of 46, in 1867. In modern times the oldest winner has been Roberto de Vicenzo of the Argentine, at the age of 44.

Hang loose, we are told, at address; not tense, taut or contorted.

--Swing Thought No. 1.

28

29

30

31

1934-Michael Bonallack, born in Essex. Currently secretary of the Royal and Ancient Golf Club of St. Andrews. Won the Amateur Championship five times between 1961 and 1970; won the English Amateur Championship five times between 1962 and 1968. Played nine times in Walker Cup matches against the U.S.A., twice as captain.

1

2

3

The Ryder Cup was named after a golf enthusiast named Samuel Ryder who, in the 1920s, had made a fortune selling seeds for gardening in penny packets. Ryder, who hailed from St. Albans, conceived of the idea of an official match between the professional golfing associations of Britain and the United States after attending an unofficial match played between the two countries at Sunningdale in 1926. Ryder presented a trophy for a match to be played every second

FOR AMERICANS ONLY

The difference between the Ryder Cup matches between the professionals of the British Isles and the United States and two unofficial matches which preceded them (at Gleneagles Hotel in 1921 and at Sunningdale in 1926) was that, in those two matches, the U.S. team included players of British birth who had emigrated to America. For the Ryder Cup places in the U.S. team were for American-born players only.

year, and that is the trophy still competed for today. Ryder had his own private 9 hole course at St. Albans and his own personal professional, Abe Mitchell, who was one of Britain's top tournament professionals at that time. Mitchell was the model for the golfer shown in the address position on the top of the Ryder Cup trophy. The first Ryder Cup match was staged in the United States in 1927.

Originally the Ryder Cup was a two day event, with foursome matches played the first day, and singles matches the second day, both over 36 holes. It is now a three-day event, with a mixture of foursome, four-ball and singles matches, all decided over 18 holes.

THREE WINS IN 50 YEARS

In the first 50 years of the Ryder Cup match British P.G.A. teams won on only three occasions: at Moortown, Leeds in 1929, at Southport and Ainsdale in 1933, and at Lindrick, Yorkshire in 1957; and never in the United States. In 1979 a European team replaced the British P.G.A. team and suffered three consecutive defeats before beating the Americans at The Belfry in 1985 and again in the United States two years later (the first time that an American team had been beaten at home in the Ryder Cup). The 1989 match at The Belfry was halved, enabling the home team to retain the trophy, before the Americans regained the trophy by the narrowest of margins at Kiawah Island in 1991.

Is your posture, at address, good? Is your abdomen UP?

-Swing Thought No. 2.

JANUARY

4

5

6

1957-Nancy Lopez, born in California. One of the outstanding U.S. women professionals of the past 15 years, including victories in the U.S. Women's Open (twice) and the U.S.L.P.G.A. Championships (three times). She won two Colgate European Opens played in Britain and has won over 40 U.S.L.P.G.A.

7

1935-Janet Wright (nee Robertson), born Glasgow. Four times winner of Scottish women's championship. Played in four Curtis Cup matches against the U.S.A.

8

9

10

ADAMS AT PINEHURST

After the playing of the 1951 Ryder Cup match at Pinehurst, North Carolina, the golf correspondent of a Scottish evening newspaper who attended the event wrote: "I had been forewarned about American ticket-checkers and their refusal to be humbugged. But I never anticipated finding them so aggressively efficient that a playing member of the British team would be told 'Pay up (four dollars) or get out', while the Ryder Cup was in progress. Yet that did happen at Pinehurst in the foursomes. James Adams was the 'victim'. John Panton (Adams's partner) had to drive at the second hole. Instead of walking back to the tee Adams, myself alongside, skirted the crowd outside the ropes to move down the side of the fairway. A huskily-built checker barred the way. After a glance at my press badge he concentrated on Adams. The genial Anglo-Scot pointed out that he did not have a badge and explained who he was. I corroborated. The checker was unimpressed. 'Player or not' he said in effect 'you must have a ticket' and he waved a bundle of them

THE 1951 BRITISH P.G.A. TEAM ABOARD THE QUEEN MARY

pointedly under Adams's nose. The gallery streamed on but the checker barred the Scot's way and no official appeared to be in sight. The situation was becoming extremely awkward when Adams suddenly remembered that he had in his pocket an inscribed billfold clip presented to him, and other members of the British team, by the U.S.P.G.A. at a function in New York. He pulled it out. The checker examined it and then, somewhat doubtfully, let us pass. Adams had to hustle to catch up with the gallery and others who were waiting for him to play and who were wondering where he had disappeared to. Thereafter Adams kept within the ropes, where the checkers did not operate!" (The checkers, incidentally, were employees of the world famous Pinkerton detective agency.)

N.B. The golf correspondent did not mention that he was in the process of reaching for his wallet to buy a ticket for Adams when the player produced the billfold clip.

11

1952-Ben Crenshaw, born in Texas. Winner of the 1984 U.S. Masters Tournament, after having been twice runner-up. Twice runner-up in the Open Championship in 1978 and 1979.

12

13

1964-Ronan Rafferty, born Northern Ireland. Winner, 1979, of British Boys Championship. Has played against the U.S.A. both as an amateur (Walker Cup) and professional (Ryder Cup).

14

1944-Graham Marsh, born Western Australia. Winner in 1977 of Colgate World Match-Play Championship.

15

16

17

WALK-OUT BY SNEAD

When an event known as the North and South Open was staged at Pinehurst, North Carolina in the week following the 1951 Ryder Cup match there, some of the members of the U.S. team (including Ben Hogan) declined to stay to compete. One who did was Sam Snead, one of the greatest golfers of that era, but he, for reasons best known to himself, holed out on the 18th in the second round ahead of his two playing partners (Open champion Max Faulkner and amateur Dick Chapman) and promptly left the course instead of waiting to compete in the two final rounds. At the same time Snead was known as *"Slammin' Sam"* because of his prodigious hitting. Following the walk-out the American golf writers attending the event re-named him *"Scramming Sam"*. Following the departure of Snead and other U.S. Ryder Cup players from this event before its completion the daily newssheet of the leading hotel at Pinehurst carried the following:

Ten little Yankee Boys, playing for the Cup,

Headed for the North & South, on the up and up.

Having won the Ryder Cup, some didn't want to strive,

They took off for richer spots, and then there were five.

Five little Ryder Cuppers, paying more and more,

One had a good excuse, and then there were four.

One said he had a pain, and then there were three.

Three little Ryder Cuppers, (we think that's too few),

One said "It's rough out there", and then there were two.

Two little Ryder Cuppers, with Sammy in the sun,

He couldn't take what comes - and then there was one.

One little Ryder Cupper upholds his country's fame,

So more power to him - Ransom is his name.

FIRST FOREIGN WINNER

The first non-British player to win the Open Championship was Arnaud Massy of France. He did so at Hoylake in 1907, with the famous Triumvirate in the field. He had competed in the event for several years before the victory and in the two years prior to his success had finished tied for fifth place and sixth.

HOTEL EMPLOYEE GOLFERS

At the time of the 1951 Ryder Cup match in Pinehurst, North Carolina, members of the British P.G.A. team discovered that the majority of the employees at the resort's top hotel, the Carolinas, were golf-minded. On most afternoons, at 2.15 pm., when they went off duty, there was usually a mad scamper from the employees' quarters to the first tee of one of the resort's four courses. There was a waitress who scored consistently in the mid-70s and a chef who frequently broke 70. This was the reason why so many of the employees, who hailed from some of the northern states in the U.S., returned to Pinehurst year after year for the eight-month season.

18

19

20

21

1940-Jack Nicklaus, born Ohio. One of four players who has won all four major titles open to professionals - the Open (three times), the U.S. Open (four times), the U.S. Masters (six times) and the U.S.P.G.A. (five times), a total of 18 in all, which is a record. Also won U.S. Amateur Championship twice.

22

23

24

1947-"Jumbo" Osaki, born in Japan. Three times winner of Japan Open and four times winner of Japan P.G.A.

GOLF HOTELS AS THEY WERE

The Gleneagles and Turnberry Hotels, and their championship golf courses, created by the former London, Midland and Scottish Railway Company, were for a number of years public property following the nationalisation of the railways after the Second World War. They are now back in private ownership. The accompanying sketches show how they advertised forty years ago.

Delightful for Holiday Golf

TURNBERRY
HOTEL
A Y R S H I R E

The famous resort and renowned Ailsa Golf Course on Scotland's Sunny West Coast

•

Enquiries for accommodation will receive the personal attention of the Resident Manager

PLAY-OFF CHANGES IN THE OPEN

Until 1963 any play-off for the title in the Open Championship had to be decided over 36 holes. That year Bob Charles, the New Zealand left-hander, won the title in a play-off with Phil Rodgers (U.S.A.). Thereafter the play-off was over 18 holes, followed, if necessary, by sudden death. More recently the play-off was reduced to 4 holes, followed by sudden death. When Mark Calcavecchia won the titles at Royal Troon in 1989 he did so in a 4-hole play-off with Greg Norman (Australia) and Wayne Grady (Australia).

GLENEAGLES
HOTEL
P E R T H S H I R E

for luxury leisure

Open from Easter to the end of October

•

Enquiries for accommodation will receive the personal attention of the Resident Manager

TOOTING BEC CUP

This trophy was presented to the Professional Golfers' Association in 1901 and is now awarded annually to the member born or resident in Great Britain or Ireland with the lowest score in any single round in the Open Championship.

VARDON TROPHY

The Harry Vardon Trophy is awarded annually to the player who finishes top of the order of merit table on the P.G.A. European Tour.

BRAID-TAYLOR MEMORIAL MEDAL

The Braid-Taylor Memorial Medal is an award to commemorate two of the three players of the Triumvirate (Vardon being the third) and is presented annually to the member of the Professional Golfers' Association born or resident in Great Britain or Ireland who finishes highest in the Open Championship.

25

26

27

28

29

30

1955-Curtis Strange, born Virginia. Won U.S. Open 1988-89. 1957-Payne Stewart born Missouri. Won U.S. Open 1991; won U.S.P.G.A. Championship 1989.

31

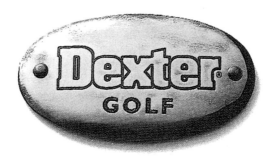

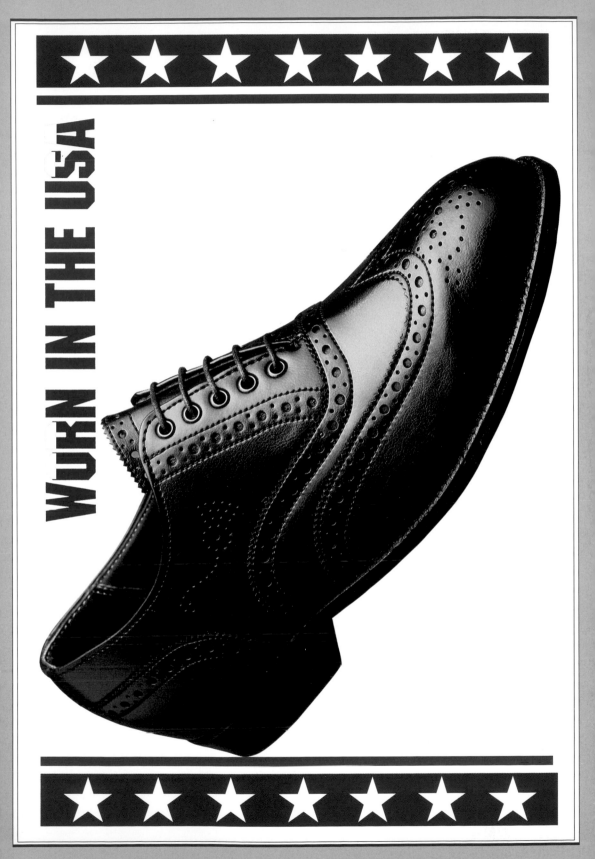

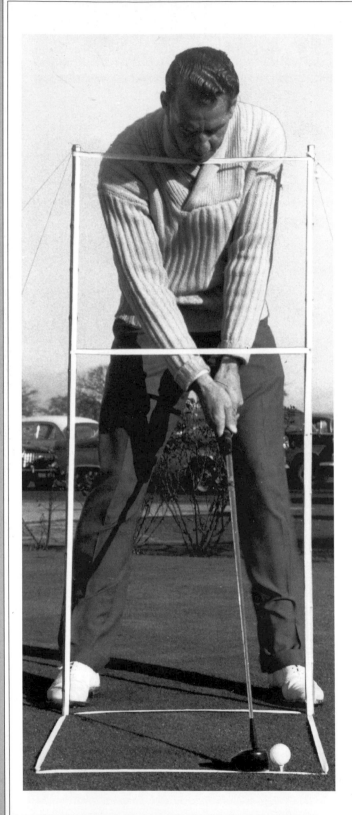

SWING AIDS

Over the years a very large number of swing aids have been offered to golfers. The accompanying photograph is of Eric Lester, a successful tournament player some 30 years ago, and shows him demonstrating an aid for getting the golfer to set up correctly at address, with the ball opposite the left foot instep, the feet parallel to the intended line of flight and the shoulders and lower forearms also lined up parallel to the intended line of flight.

BRITISH SUCCESSES IN U.S. OPEN

Only three British players resident in Britain have won the U.S. Open Championship. Harry Vardon was the first to do so in 1900; Ted Ray the second in 1920; and Tony Jacklin the third in 1970, when he was the holder of the Open Championship title. In 1988 Nick Faldo tied with Curtis Strange for first place but was beaten by the American in an 18 hole play-off. However the early years of the U.S. Open were dominated by British-born professionals who had emigrated to the United States. They included Willie Anderson who won the event four times. Three of his wins were in consecutive years, an achievement that has never been matched in the event.

FEBRUARY

1

2

3

4

1912-Byron Nelson, born Texas. Winner of the U.S. Open in 1939; winner of the U.S.P.G.A. Championship in 1940 and 1945; winner of the U.S. Masters in 1937 and 1942. During 1945 had eleven consecutive wins on the U.S. Tour and 18 for the year.

5

1966-Jose Maria Olazabal, born Spain. Before turning professional won British Boys Championship in 1983 and the Amateur Championship in 1984. Was runner-up in U.S. Masters in 1991. Has played against U.S.A. in three Ryder Cup matches.

6

7

LADIES' GOLF

The earliest known reference to a woman playing golf dates from 1568, when Mary, Queen of Scots, was censured for playing golf near Musselburgh shortly after the murder of her husband, Lord Darnley. The earliest known reference to a woman's golf competition dates from 1810 at Musselburgh; it was played in January 1811. The Ladies' Golf Club at St. Andrews was formed in 1867 and

the one at Westward Ho! in Devon, started in June 1868. In both instances, the women played on putting courses. It was not until the 1870s that ladies began to play with a set of clubs on short courses.

In the 1991 Ryder Cup match at Kiawah Island, Bernhard Langer (Germany) had a putt of a few feet on the last green to enable the European team to halve the match overall and so retain the trophy. He missed. It was not the only occasion on which the outcome of an important international match has hinged on a final putt. In the 1936 Curtis Cup match played over the King's Course at Gleneagles Hotel between the women amateurs of Britain and the United States, everything hinged on a last green putt of some nine feet for the "baby" of the home team, Miss Jessie Anderson, the daughter of a professional in Perth. Miss Anderson holed the putt and so gave the home team a halved match with the holders. Miss Anderson, now Mrs. George Valentine, went on to win the British women's amateur championship three times, and the Scottish women's amateur championship six times, and to play in another six Curtis Cup matches.

"BABE" ZAHARIAS

The major attraction at the 1947 British Ladies' Championship at Gullane, East Lothian, was the appearance of the American "Babe" Zaharias who, in 1932, had established three world records in the Olympic Games. She had subsequently taken up golf and following numerous success, won the U.S. women's title in 1946. Spectators at Gullane were overawed by her power. When asked what she did when she wanted an extra long drive, she replied smilingly "Honey, I just loosen my girdle a trifle." She won the title, subsequently turned professional and as such, won major titles, including the U.S. Women's Open in two consecutive years, when she was named the greatest female athlete of the half-century. She died in 1956 from cancer.

FEBRUARY

8

9

1958-Sandy Lyle, born Shrewsbury. Winner of the Open Championship in 1985; winner of U.S. Masters in 1988. 1949-Bernard Gallacher, born Bathgate, Scotland. Played for Scotland as an amateur before turning professional. Played eight times against the U.S.A. in Ryder Cup matches and non-playing captain in 1991. Four times Scottish professional champion.

10

1955-Greg Norman, Born Queensland, Australia. Winner of Open Championship in 1986. Has been runner-up in the U.S. Open, the U.S.P.G.A. Championship and the U.S. Masters (twice).

11

12

1953-Des Smyth, born Drogheda. Twice Ryder Cup matches against U.S.A. Professional since 1973.

13

1918-Patty Berg, born Minneapolis. Winner of 1938 U.S. women's amateur and 1946 U.S. women's open. 57 wins on U.S.L.P.G.A. Tour.

14

The original name of the Royal and Ancient Golf Club of St. Andrews was the St. Andrews Society of Golfers, founded in 1754.

HOW A ROUND BECAME 18 HOLES

It is not known how and when 18 holes became generally accepted as being the test for a round of golf. In earlier days golf courses had different numbers of holes. The Links of Leith, on which clubs like the Honourable Company of Edinburgh Golfers and the Royal Burgess Golfing Society used to hold their competitions some 250 years ago, consisted of 5 holes. During the ensuing century there were courses in Scotland that consisted of 5, 6, 7, 13, 15 and even 25 holes. A match at Royal Blackheath used to consist of three rounds of 7 holes. When the Open Championship began at Prestwick in 1860 the course measured only 12 holes and the championship consisted of three rounds of play, making 36 holes (the equivalent of two rounds of 18 holes). Whether or not this was done because 18 holes was already being accepted on the east coast of Scotland as measure of a round of golf, is not clear. But when the Royal and Ancient Golf Club of St. Andrews and the Honourable Company of Edinburgh Golfers subsequently joined Prestwick as organiser

of the championship, this brought in an 18 hole test, 9 holes out and 9 holes back, using 11 greens, (at St. Andrews) and a 9 hole test (Musselburgh). This, with the growing influence of St. Andrews in golf, could have paved the way for 18 holes being accepted as the standard. It should be noted that in 1883, Prestwick became an 18 hole course, very different from the original. To this day the Shiskine course at Blackwaterfoot, on the Isle of Arran in the estuary of the River Clyde, which dates from 1896, consists of 12 holes...

WHEN ST. ANDREWS HAD 22 HOLES

There was a time when the links of St. Andrews now know as the Old Course (to distinguish it from the New Course and also the Eden and Jubilee courses) had 12 holes. The first 11 were played straight out to near the Eden estuary and then the first ten greens were played as those of the inward holes, together with a single green beside the clubhouse, making a round of 22 holes in all. When two groups of players reached a green at the same time those playing the outward hole were permitted to hole out first. Then, in 1764 (almost a century before the Open Championship began) the first 4 holes were converted into 2, which meant that a round became 18 holes.

OLD COURSE, ST. ANDREWS, 1862

Are you crouching over the ball at address?
-Swing Thought No. 8.

FEBRUARY

15

16

17

18
1922-Joe Carr, born Dublin. Winner of Amateur Championship 1953, 1958 and 1960. Six times Irish amateur champion. Ten appearances in Walker Cup matches against the U.S. Once semi-finalist in U.S. Amateur and twice leading amateur in Open Championship. Captain of the R. and A. 1991-92. 1947-Jose Maria Canizares, born Madrid. Has played four times in Ryder Cup matches against the U.S.A. Turned professional in 1967.

19

20

21
1945-Maurice Bembridge, born Worksop. Four times winner in Ryder Cup matches against U.S.A. Leading British player in 1968 Open Championship.

CHALLENGE MATCHES

The first recorded challenge match took place in 1843 and it must have been a marathon as it was decided over twenty rounds - 360 holes. It was between Allan Robertson of St. Andrews and Willie Dunn of Musselburgh and ended with Robertson two rounds up with one round to play. During the next fifteen years a number of other challenge matches took place and on most occasions the sum at stake was £100, a considerable amount of money in those days. There was one match in which Robertson and Tom Morris, both of St. Andrews, played the Musselburgh brothers Dunn for £400 over three different courses, with the St. Andrews pair emerging the narrowest of winners. Frequently there was considerable partisanship displayed at these matches by spectators, some of whom probably had side bets on the outcome, and it is recorded that this happened when Willie Park and Tom Morris engaged in a series of six matches, each for £100. When the fifth of the matches took place at Musselburgh, spectators interfered so often with Morris's ball that the referee stopped play and he and Morris adjourned to a nearby hostelry. After waiting some time on the course Park sent a message to the effect that, if they did not return for a resumption of play, he would complete the remaining holes and claim the stakes, which he did. Towards the end of the last century and the start of the present, there were a considerable number of challenge matches in which the Triumvirate (Harry Vardon, J.H. Taylor and James Braid) as well as other leading professionals of the day, featured.

GOFF, and the *Man*, I sing, who, em'lous, plies
The jointed club; whose balls invade the skies;
Who from *Edina's* tow'rs, his peaceful home,
In quest of fame o'er *Letha's* plains did roam.
Long toil'd the hero, on the verdant field,
Strain'd his stout arm the weighty club to wield;
Such toils it costs, such labours to obtain
The bays of conquest, and the bowl to gain.

-From *The Goff*,
Thomas Mathison, c.1743

ALLAN ROBERTSON AND
TOM MORRIS

Are your hands too close to or too far from your thighs?

-Swing Thought No. 9.

FEBRUARY

22

23

24

25

26

27

1902-Gene Sarazen, born New York. First player to win all the four modern "majors" - the Open, the U.S. Open, the U.S. Masters and the U.S.P.G.A. Championship.

28

1931-Peter Alliss, born Berlin. Son of famous British professional. Played eight times in Ryder Cup matches against U.S.A. Now TV commentator.

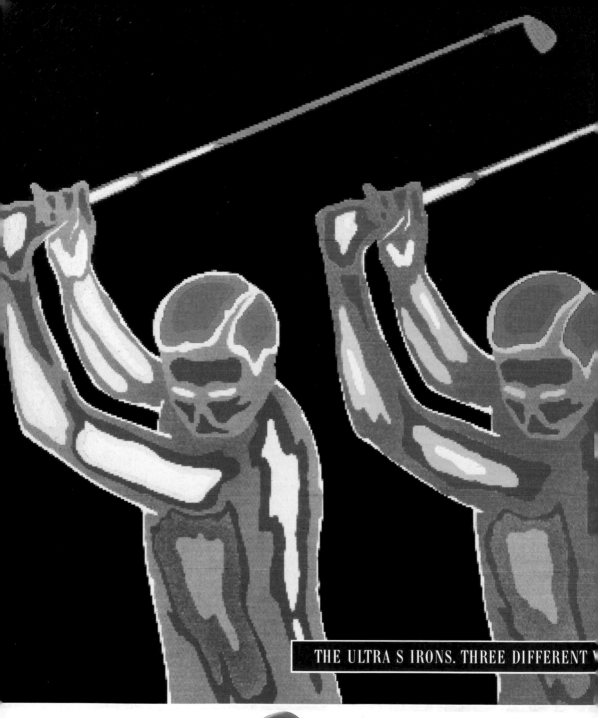

THE ULTRA S IRONS. THREE DIFFERENT

Our designers' brains have been glowing incandescent recently.

How can we transfer more of your natural energy to the ball? That's the question.

Last year's solution, the Firestick graphite shaft, was the hottest news in golfing circles for decades.

This year we've cast our minds back to the problem again. And come up with the Firestick Steels.

The graphite technology adapted to metal shaf producing the Ultra S Iron.

We took a long, cold look at the competiti We noted how limited the choice of shaft was f different kinds of swing. That they offer thre stiffnesses is fine. But it's not enough.

What is then?

For a start, we added three different kickpoin

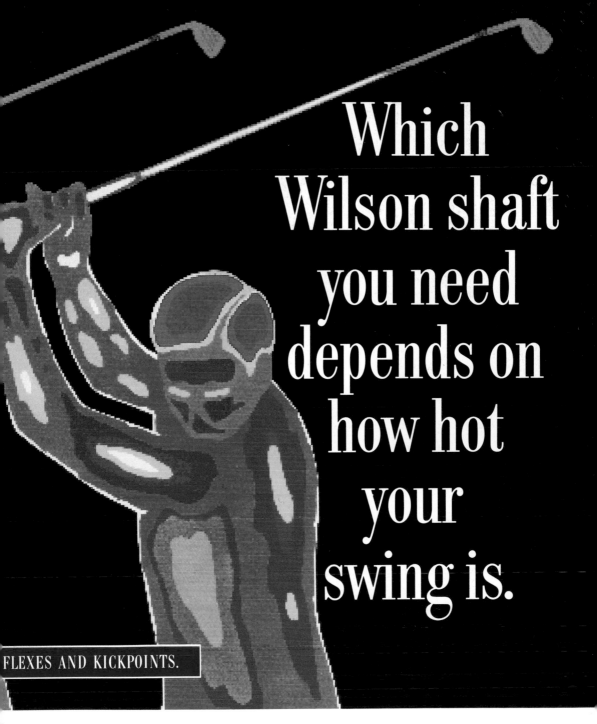

Which Wilson shaft you need depends on how hot your swing is.

For regular swings our kickpoint is lower, thus ving you the loft you need.

The fastest swingers in town get the other extreme, igh kickpoint, to compensate for their strength.

We also offer you three different shaft weights. e heavier your swing, the heavier the steel.

Then we matched these gunsmoke finished shafts the CAD/CAM designed Ultra S head with its system

45° weight distribution. And the result? The sharpest slivers of cold steel on the fairway.

John Daly's already using Wilson Ultra S Irons. As are twenty other PGA Tour players on both sides of the Atlantic.

A fact that makes our designers glow with pride.

Wilson
MADE TO WIN

AMATEURS IN CHALLENGE MATCHES

In the latter part of the last century amateurs could, or did, participate in challenge matches as well as professionals. One who did so, following in the footsteps of his father, was John Ball, who was subsequently to become an eight times winner of the Amateur Championship (a record for the event) when that event began in 1887. Ball, whose base was Hoylake, home of Royal Liverpool Golf Club, was apparently an outstandingly accomplished golfer at an early age, so much so that in 1885 when he was 20, a challenge was issued from Hoylake on his behalf to play any other amateur in the world. This challenge was taken up by a Scot, Douglas Stewart Rolland of Elie, Fife, who from the age of 13 had worked as a stonemason and who was at the time of match, 23. Rolland got financial backing for the match, which surprised many because Ball already had the reputation if being invincible. The match consisted of two rounds at Elie and two rounds at Hoylake. To the astonishment of the Ball supporters, the Englishman finished the first leg at Elie, 9 holes down. He won back only 1 hole in the subsequent first round at Hoylake, but had no answer to Rolland's superior skill and was finally beaten by 11 to 10. Ball took this defeat very much to heart, so much so that, in any effort to restore his standing and ego, he challenged the Scot to play another match the following day at Hoylake over two rounds. It looked as though Ball was to get his revenge when he stood 5 up with 6 to play, but the Scot, who by all accounts had a magnificent physique, then won the remaining 6 holes to beat the English player once more. Heartened by this achievement Rolland turned professional, became attached to an English club and played with considerable success in professional tournaments and challenge matches.

When in 1894, Willie Park Junior challenged the world it was Rolland who took up the challenge and again won, this time over 36 holes at Sandwich, for a £100 stake. Rolland's ability was underlined by the fact that he finished joint runner-up in the 1884 Open Championship. He was also runner-up to J.H. Taylor in 1894.

JOHN BALL

MARCH

1

2

1958-Ian Woosnam, born Oswestry. Winner of U.S. Masters in 1991. Has played five times in Ryder Cup matches against the U.S.A. Has been runner-up in the U.S. Open and third in the Open.

3

1920-Julius Boros, born Connecticut. Winner of the U.S. Open in 1952 and 1963. Won U.S.P.G.A. Championship in 1968 at the age of 48. Four times in Ryder Cup matches.

4

5

6

7

GOLF AT HIGH ALTITUDE

Writing in *A Summer in High Asia* Captain F.E.S. Blair described how, in crossing into Tibet, he camped at a spot carpeted with short, bright green turf, on the edge of a lake. He wrote, "Being a golf enthusiast I had brought a driver and a putter with me and, having made a hole in the short turf, I instituted a competition for the camp. I should think that this was the first time that the Royal game had been played at an elevation of upwards of 16,000 feet."

NEW LEADER BOARD FACILITY

At the 1992 Open Championship at Muirfield a completely new set of leader boards, which cost over £100,000, provided at every hole up-to-date scoring information. These supplemented other major scoreboards placed around the course.

DALY'S MIGHTY HITTING

On the practice ground at Muirfield for the 1992 Open Championship an 18ft-high fence was erected at a distance of 280 yards to keep the shots of John Daly, the reigning U.S.P.G.A. champion, in play. But, when Daly arrived on the scene, his drives flew over the fence, and so the hitting area had to be moved back even further.

BRADSHAW AND THE BROKEN BOTTLE

In the 1949 Open Championship at Royal St. George's, Sandwich, Harry Bradshaw had the misfortune at one hole to find his ball had finished inside part of a broken bottle. As the rules were at that time, he had to play the ball as it lay or be penalised for lifting it out. He played the ball as it lay in the bottle but, inevitable, only sent it a few yards, effectively losing a stroke. He then finished in a tie for first place with Bobby Locke of South Africa, only to lose to Locke in the ensuing 36-hole play-off. Twenty-eight years earlier, in the 1921 Open at St. Andrews, there was a first-place tie between Jock Hutchison, a Scot who had settled in the U.S.A., and an amateur, Roger Wethered, who, in the third round, had incurred a penalty stroke by treading on his ball while walking backwards to study the line of shot.

There were 17,00 grandstand seats for spectators at the 1992 Open Championship at Muirfield - more than ever before - and 15,000 of these were free of charge, erected at prime viewing locations on 12 of the holes.

RULE XXIII
If ye player's ball strike an opponent's caddie . . . . ye opponent shall lose ye hole . . . and perhaps ye caddie)

RÈGLE XXIII
Si la balle d'un joueur...
frappe le caddie d'un adversaire...
l'adversaire perdra le bénéfice du trou...
et peut-être le caddie...

Left foot turned out slightly and right foot square is standard.

-Swing Thought No. 11.

MARCH

8

9

1950-Andy North, born Wisconsin. Winner of the U.S. Open in 1978 and 1985.

10

11

12

13

14

1936-Bob Charles, born New Zealand. Winner of Open Championship in 1963, becoming first left-hander and first New Zealander to do so.

The diameter of the golf hole is 4¼ inches.

WHEN THE SMALL BALL "DIED"
For almost 60 years there were two different standard golf balls. There was the 1.68in. (large) ball which was the standard

in the North American continent and the 1.62in. (small) ball which was standard for the rest of the world but illegal in North America. January 1990 marked the eventual demise of the small ball. The Royal and Ancient Golf Club announced as follows:- "With the steady and, in most countries, rapid decline in the use of the 1.62in. ("small") ball the R. and A. has been considering changing to the 1.68in. ("large") ball for some time, but has held off from doing so mainly because of the large number of Japanese golfers still using the small ball. With the use of the small ball in Japan now dropping steadily, and in most other countries now being at 10 per cent or less, it seems an appropriate time to make this change."

A number of Presidents of the United States have had specially autographed golf balls made, chiefly for giving as presents to close golfing friends. Two who have done so have been Richard Nixon and Ronald Reagan.

CHANGING SPONSORSHIP
In the years between the two world wars and for a period after the Second World War, almost all the professional tournaments played in Britain were sponsored by golf ball firms or national newspapers. There were tournaments that bore the ball names of *Dunlop*, *Silver King*, *Penfold* and *North British* and others were promoted by such newspapers as the Daily Mail, the News Chronicle and the News of the World, whose match-play tournament began in 1903 and came to be recognised, in time, as the match-play championship of the Professional Golfers' Association. That newspaper's sponsorship only ended in 1968.

A HOLE CUTTER

15

1954-Hollis Stacy, born Georgia. Winner of U.S.
women's open in 1977, 1978 and 1984.

16

17

18

1915-Mrs Jessie Valentine (nee Anderson), born Perth. Won the British women open
amateur championship in 1937, 1955 and 1958. Winner of the Scottish women's
amateur championship in 1938, 1939, 1951 1953, 1955 and 1956. Won New Zealand
championship in 1935. Played in seven Curtis Cup matches against the U.S.A. Was
British girls champion in 1933.

19

20

1959-Dale Reid, born Fife. Has won more than
20 tournaments on the European tour for
women professionals.

21

WHEN GOLF WAS BANNED BY LAW

Golf was already so popular in Scotland in the middle of the 15th century that in 1457, the parliament of King James II declared the game illegal because it was felt that it was interfering with the practice of archery, considered necessary in case of a war with England. So anyone caught playing golf was fined or imprisoned. Despite this edict the game continued to flourish, particularly with noblemen on links courses by the sea. Later that century the introduction of gunpowder made archery for warfare virtually obsolete and in due course golf could once more be played without legal punishment.

ROYAL GOLFER AT ST. ANDREWS

When the Duke of York played a round of golf over the Old Course, St. Andrews, in August 1992, it was the first golf played there by a member of the Royal Family since 1937 when the Duke's great-uncle, the late Duke of Kent, drove off the first tee to play himself into office as captain of the Royal and Ancient Golf Club of St. Andrews. The Duke plays to a handicap of 16.

CHARLES I, PLAYING ON LEITH LINKS, RECEIVES NEWS OF THE IRISH REBELLION

SHOEMAKER PARTNERS PRINCE

When James II (of England) and VII (of Scotland) was Prince of Wales he became involved in a challenge match with two English noblemen to be played over the Links of Leith. Benefitting from advice given to him, the Prince engaged as his partner a poor shoemaker named John Paterson, who had the reputation of being skilled at the game. The match was duly played and the Prince and his partner won. The Prince gave the stakes to Paterson who used the money to build a house in the Canongate which stood until 1961, while his business as a shoemaker, under royal patronage, flourished.

Two centuries after the ban on golf was first imposed in Scotland, King Charles I of Great Britain was playing golf on the links of Leith, near Edinburgh in 1642, when he received the news of a rebellion in Ireland.

Is the ball opposite your left armpit at address?
-Swing Thought No. 13.

22

1953-Peter McEvoy, born London. Winner of Amateur Championship in 1977 and 1978 and twice leading amateur in the Open Championship. Has played in five Walker Cup matches against the U.S.A.

23

24

25

26

27

28

Auchterlonies
of
St. Andrews

2-4 Golf Place, St. Andrews
Fife, Scotland
Tel: 0334 - 73253

As St. Andrews
is to Golf
Auchterlonies is to
St. Andrews

OLDEST GOLF CLUBS

The eleven clubs below are the only ones known to have come into existence before the end of the 18th century. The earliest written evidence of the existence of the Royal Burgess G.S. of Edinburgh is 1773, but it is believed that it was in existence prior to that date and 1735 is claimed in the Chronicles of the Society. It is believed that golf was first played at Royal Blackheath in 1608, after the Scottish King, James VI, ascended the English throne but written evidence dates the club from 1787. The Honourable Company will celebrate its 250th anniversary in 1994.

LINKS AT ST. ANDREWS

- ■ Royal Burgess G.S.   1735
- ■ Honourable Company of Edinburgh Golfers   1744
- ■ Royal and Ancient Golf Club of St. Andrews   1754
- ■ Bruntsfield Links   1761
- ■ Royal Musselburgh   1774

- ■ Royal Aberdeen   1780
- ■ Crail   1786
- ■ Glasgow   1787
- ■ Royal Blackheath   1787
- ■ Dunbar   1794
- ■ Burntisland   1797

MEDAL DAY AT BLACKHEATH

29

30

31

1931-Miller Barber, born Louisiana. Winner of eleven events on the U.S.P.G.A. Tour and more than 20 on the U.S. senior tour.

1

2

3

4

1939-JoAnne Carner, born Washington. Five times U.S. women's amateur champion and twice U.S. women's open champion. Has had over 40 professional tournament wins.

CHAMPIONSHIP COURSES - THEN AND NOW

In the last 70 years championship courses in Britain have only been extended by some 400 yards. So, with the tremendous improvements that have been made in ball and club manufacturing, resulting in the golf ball being hit ever-increasing distances, these courses now play much shorter, relatively, than they did in the 1920s. That fact is reflected in the way in which scoring has come down over the years. Back in 1925, to give two examples, the Old Course at St. Andrews was already 6572 yards in length and Muirfield 6675 yards.

following year, twelve rounds of the Aberdeen links and thereafter to walk ten miles, all within 24 hours. On the following 6th July it was noted: "This day Mr. Bloxham appeared to play the twelve rounds and walk the ten miles he backed himself to do at the last dinner. He began work at six in the morning and finished his twelve rounds between 8 and 9 pm. He afterwards walked from the first milestone on the Deeside road to the sixth at Milltimber and back to the Schoolhill, where he arrived at about 1.15 pm, thus triumphantly performing his task with some hours to spare." At that time the Aberdeen course consisted of 15 holes so

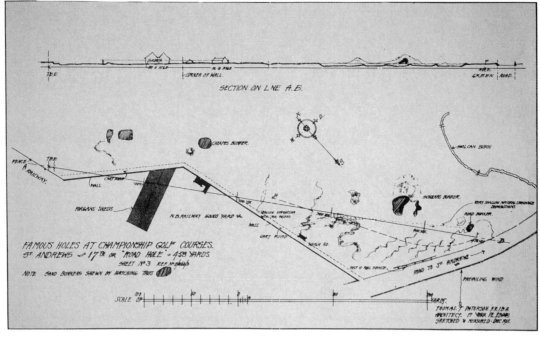

A SKETCH OF THE ROAD HOLE ON THE OLD COURSE AT ST. ANDREWS IN 1911, WHICH WAS PART OF A SURVEY CARRIED OUT BY GOLF MONTHLY MAGAZINE

AN UNUSUAL WAGER

The records of the Aberdeen Golf Club in 1874 show that one of the members during a September club function, backed himself to play, before the club's autumn meeting the

Bloxham played 180 holes which approximated to thirty two-miles that he walked on the links. It was noted that Bloxham was in such good form that in his final round, which he played with the club secretary and in which he conceded a stroke a hole, he beat the secretary by 14 holes, only the last hole being halved. Prior to this achievement Bloxham had proved he had the stamina for such an undertaking by playing sixteen rounds of Musselburgh (a 9 hole course) against professional Bob Ferguson, a three-times Open champion, in 1874, starting at 6 am and finishing at 7 pm.

5

6

7

8

9

1957-Severiano Ballesteros, born Pedrena, Spain. Winner of Open Championship in 1979, 1984 and 1988. Winner of U.S. Masters in 1980 and 1983. Has had 70 championship and tournament wins worldwide since 1976. Has played six times in Ryder Cup matches against the U.S.

10

11

1936-Belle Robertson (nee McCorkindale), born Mull of Kintyre. Winner of British women's open amateur championship, 1981. Scottish champion six times.

TWO DIFFERENT METHODS

After players from the United States (three of them British-born) had won all but one of the thirteen Open Championships played between 1921 and 1933, Donald Mathieson, owner/editor of the magazine *Golf Monthly*, wrote to Victor East asking if the latter was of the opinion that American methods of stroke-making were superior to those of the British. East was an Australian-born professional who had settled in the United States, who had played in the Open Championship and who had the reputation in his day of being an outstanding judge of the golf swing. East's answer to the query was "Yes" and he supplemented that with the following: "In the average the American method differs from that of the British. The former, during ball impact, maintains a squareness of the clubface to the line of play to a greater extent than the latter, and arranges this sustained squareness without loss of clubhead speed, or, in other words, without sacrificing distance. The different manner of meeting, and, as it were, of 'going through' the ball, is attributable to a changed method of operating the earlier process of the swing. The British method of developing the early motions is to have a considerable movement of the hands, wrists and forearms; these actions are of a kind which could be said to have a rotating effect on the clubface. The American method more generally avoids the free or separate use of these localised movements of the hands, wrists and forearms, and the swing gets under way with a spontaneous co-ordination of all the working parts of the entire figure." That was sixty years ago!

*"THREE POSITIONS OF GRIP",
THE BADMINTON LIBRARY, GOLF, 1890*

EXHIBITION MATCHES

For more than a century challenge matches were an important part of golf, the last one of any note being played in 1952. Thereafter, for some years, exhibition matches in aid of charity were a regular feature in Britain. These were normally played on a Sunday when professional tournaments still had a Friday (and subsequently a Saturday) finish. Then, when schedules were changed, so that important professional events were played to finish on a Sunday, these exhibition matches came to an end. Three players who took a prominent part in many of these exhibition matches were Max Faulkner, the 1951 Open Champion, Dai Rees and Ken Bousfield.

Do you avoid dropping your chin into the chest?
-Swing Thought No. 16.

APRIL

12

13

14

1923-Robert de Vicenzo, born Buenos Aires. Winner of Open Championship in 1967 at the age of 44. In 1968 missed chance of a play-off in the U.S. Masters by signing his final round card for one stroke more (at one hole) than he actually took.

15

16

17

18

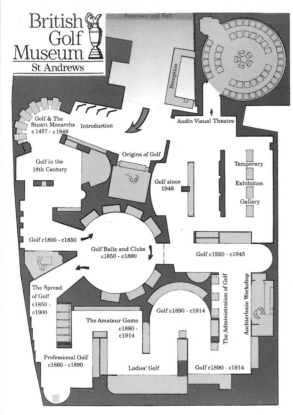

Golf & The
Stuart Monarchs Introduction
c 1457 - c 1649

Golf in the
18th Century

Origins of Golf

Golf since
1946

Temporary

Exhibition

Gallery

Golf c1800 - c1850

Golf Balls and Clubs
c1850 - c1890

Golf c1920 - c1945

The Spread
of Golf
c1850 -
c1900

Golf c1890 - c1914

The Amateur Game
c1880 -
c1914

The Administration of Golf

Auchterlonie Workshop

Professional Golf
c1860 - c1890

Ladies' Golf

Golf c1890 - c1914

Entrance and Exit

Reception

Audio Visual Theatre

LAYOUT OF THE BRITISH GOLF MUSEUM

BRITISH GOLF MUSEUM

One of the most important additions to the golf scene took place in 1990 with the opening of the British Golf Museum in St. Andrews, Fife, Scotland. The museum is located only a few yards from the clubhouse of the Royal and Ancient Golf Club of St. Andrews and should be visited by anyone who has the slightest interest in the game, and even by others who could be interested to learn what golf is all about. The museum spans 500 years and it is not surprising that it has already won several awards since its opening. The accompanying sketch show the layout and gives an indication of the various aspects of the game that are featured. In the museum are twelve touchscreens containing more than 140 programme choices. At the touch of a fingertip visitors can activate accounts of dramatic matches from 1860 to the present day, biographies of famous players and championship statistics. There are also two quizzes to test the knowledge of visitors - one dealing with the rules of the game and the other with the game's history. Some of the items illustrated elsewhere in this book are among those on show in the museum.

AN EXAMPLE OF THE DISPLAYS

THE SILVER BALLS

Do you, perchance, grip too tightly with the fingers?

-Swing Thought No. 17.

APRIL

19

20

21

22

23

1938-Deane Beman, born Washington. Winner of the 1959 Amateur Championship; and winner of U.S. Amateur Championship in 1960 and 1963 before turning professional. Since 1974 commissioner of the U.S.P.G.A. Tour.

24

25

THE 1905 OPEN CHAMPIONSHIP AT ST. ANDREWS. THESE REMARKABLE PICTURES SHOW JAMES BRAID DRIVING OFF AND RECOVERING FROM THE RAILWAY LINE TWICE - THE FIRST TIME FROM THE 15TH AND THE SECOND FROM THE 16TH. THE RAILWAY LINE WAS NOT OUT OF BOUNDS IN THOSE DAYS

RAILWAY STATION FOR GOLFERS

In the days before motor car travel became commonplace, many Glasgow golfers who were members of three clubs in mid-Ayrshire, beside the coast, had the benefit of a railway station of their own (it could be called a halt) to enable them to get to and from their clubs. The station was called Gailes. It was out in what could be best described as open country, but it was within easy access of the clubhouses of three courses - Glasgow Gailes (the No. 2. course of Glasgow Golf Club), Western Gailes and Dundonald. Indeed the northbound platform was only a matter of yards from the Western Gailes clubhouse. That particular railway line provided a sterling service for golfers. The Troon station was, as it still is, only a chip shot away from the first tees of the town's three public courses (Darley, Lochgreen and Fullarton), while the Prestwick station was, and is, across the wall from the present first hole of the Prestwick golf course. At the clubhouse of the Irvine club at Bogside, adjoining the Bogside station, the clubmaster would ring a bell to let members who had finished their rounds and who were at the 19th hole, know that the train for Glasgow was approaching the station. (N.B. There is no longer a Dundonald course, but Glasgow Gailes and Western Gailes are both still in existence and have been venues for the Scottish Amateur Championship and other important national events.)

Gleneagles Hotel and its courses, was a creation of the private railway companies of the early part of the present century and it began shortly before the outbreak of the First World War, which interrupted construction. In consequence when the Glasgow Herald in 1920, promoted a match-play tournament for professionals to be played annually over the Gleneagles Hotel King's course which had been completed, the hotel was not initially ready to accommodate the players and others attending the event. The railway company, anxious to have the attractions of Gleneagles voiced abroad, solved this problem by providing accommodation in sleeper coaches which stayed in sidings at the nearby Auchterarder station, for the duration of the event.

Do you favour an overlap (Vardon), two-handed or interlock grip?

-Swing Thought No. 18.

APRIL/MAY

26

27

28

29

1947-Johnny Miller, born California. Winner of Open Championship in 1976; winner of the U.S. Open Championship in 1973. In 1974 was U.S.P.G.A. player of the year and leading money winner in the U.S.A. 1949-Mary McKenna, born Dublin. Played nine times in Curtis Cup matches against the U.S.A. between 1970 and 1986.

30

1

2

MILETA SPORTS LIMITED

Mileta Sports established in Great Britain in 1959 are one of Europe's largest manufacturers of waterproof golf suits and related golf products. All Mileta branded products are U.K. made in their own factory. The company has invested heavily in CADCAM and robotics to aid quality and design.

All our suits are waterproof, breathable, lightweight and quiet. The jacket features two pockets and a generous cut to allow ease of movement. The trouser has back and side pockets and many models feature the unique patented "press up" system. This system allows simple and easy self adjustment for differing leg lengths.

All waterproof products have machine taped seams throughout and carry a guarantee. Mileta supply their waterproof clothing to the England mens and ladies teams.

Mileta rainwear.

Waterproof – Breathable – Guaranteed

Stylish – Comfortable – Quiet in use.

Guaranteed Performance

Made in Micro-Fibre with a Cyclone Drop Liner.

Worn by the England mens and ladies teams.

Need we say more?

Cyclone is a trademark of C.V. Woven Fabrics Ltd.

Mileta Sports Ltd, Spen Vale Mills, Station Lane, Heckmondwike, West Yorkshire, England WF16 0NQ.

Please send me a full colour brochure and stockist list.

WORLD MATCH-PLAY CHAMPIONSHIP

The World Match-Play Championship, the concept of American impresario Mark McCormack and played each year since its inception in 1964 at Wentworth, was first sponsored by *Piccadilly* and subsequently by *Colgate* and then *Suntory*. The present sponsor is *Toyota*.

NO INVITATION TO MASTERS

Tom Kite did not receive an invitation to compete in the 1992 U.S. Masters Tournament though, in the view of almost everyone, he merited one. Two months later Kite, the all-time money winner of the U.S.P.G.A. Tour, won the U.S. Open, his first success in a major championship.

REMARKABLE FINISH

One of the most remarkable finishes to a major 72 hole stroke tournament for professionals ever recorded occurred in the 1992 Bell's Scottish Open over the King's Course at Gleneagles Hotel, Scotland, when Peter O'Malley, a young Australian, came from behind to win. He finished his final round with a single putt at each of the last five holes, which he played 2-3-2-3-3. In that stretch he had two eagles (one at the 310 yards 14th, the other at the par 5 18th) and three birdies. That finish gave him a final round of 62, enabling him to beat Colin Montgomerie who finished with a 65, by two strokes.

The youngest winner of the Open Championship in modern times has been Severiano Ballesteros of Spain. He was 22 when he won for the first time in 1979.

RECORD INWARD HALF SCORE

In the 1992 U.S. Masters, Mark Calcavecchia, winner of the 1989 Open Championship, had a record-breaking score of 29 for the inward nine holes in the final round. After a birdie at the 10th and par figures at the 11th and 12th, he then completed the round with six consecutive birdies. He still finished ten strokes behind the winner.

Major event venues for 1993 are Royal St. George's, Sandwich for the Open Championship in July; Baltusrol for the U.S. Open in June; and Inverness for the U.S.P.G.A. Championship in August. The U.S. Masters plays at its customary venue of Augusta, Georgia in April.

AGW OPEN CHAMPIONSHIP DINNER 1980

Guest of Honour SEVERIANO BALLESTEROS

Tragedy! Sevvy's drive is in the middle of the fairway. He likes to play his second from underneath a Rover 3,000, over a Ferrari 400 GT and bounce off a Ford Granada to within 6 inches of the pin.

Open Arms Hotel. Dirleton.   Tuesday 15th July.

3

1948-Peter Oosterhuis, born London. Dominant player in Britain for four years, winning order of merit from 1971 to 1974. Played six times in Ryder Cup matches against the U.S.A. Twice a runner-up in the Open Championship. Subsequently continued tournament career in the U.S.A. and now settled in California.

4

1928-Betsy Rawls, born South Carolina. Four times winner of U.S. women's open, with 55 career wins on the U.S.L.P.G.A. Tour. 1959-Bob Tway, born Oklahoma. Winner of 1986 U.S.P.G.A. Championship.

5

6

7

8

9

NICK FALDO IN THE OPEN

Below is Nick Faldo's record in the Open Championship since he first appeared in the field for the final stages of the event in 1976. He has never missed qualifying for the final day since. Only three times has he been out of the top 20 and only once since 1978. In the last 13 years he only been twice outside of the top 12.

- 1976 - Tied 28th
- 1977 - Tied 62nd
- 1978 - Tied 7th
- 1979 - Tied 19th
- 1980 - Tied 12th
- 1981 - Tied 11th
- 1982 - Tied 4th
- 1983 - Tied 8th
- 1984 - Tied 6th
- 1986 - Fifth
- 1987 - Winner
- 1988 - Third
- 1989 - Tied 11th
- 1990 - Winner
- 1991 - Tied 17th
- 1992 - Winner

THE MISSING YEARS

While Sir Henry Cotton (his knighthood, which he had accepted, was officially announced days after his death in December 1987) won the Open Championship three times between 1934 and 1948, there has always been speculation about how many more times he might have done so but for the interruption of the 1939-45 war during which there were six years in which the event was not played.

THE ALLISSES - FATHER AND SON

The first famous father-and-son duo were Tom Morris and his son Young Tom, who were both multiple winners of the Open Championship in the first eleven years it was played. In more recent times another famous father-and-son duo has been Percy and Peter Alliss, both in their day, outstanding tournament professionals and both Ryder Cup players against the United States. Percy Alliss was one of a number of leading British professionals in the 1920s and 1930s who were rated good enough to have been winners of the Open Championship but who never were in the period of dominance in the event by players from the United States. It was said of Percy Alliss that his putting was his Achilles heel and that, with more consistency on the greens, he could have been a champion more than once. It may be significant that his son Peter, now a distinguished TV commentator, had a number plate of "PUT 3" for his car - like father, like son. When Peter, at the age of 16, competed in the British Boys Championship at Bruntsfield Links, Edinburgh in 1946, his father was in the gallery watching play in the quarter-finals. A golf correspondent alongside the father commented on the excellence of young Peter's swing whereupon father Percy responded: "Yes, he has only one thing to learn." When asked what that was he replied: "He still has to learn to hit the ball with his posterior." (Though he used a more explicit four letter word to describe that part of his son's anatomy).

10

1951-Beverly Huke, born Great Yarmouth. Winner of English women's amateur championship in 1975; runner-up in British women's amateur championship in 1971. Turned professional in 1978.

11

12

13

14

15

16

RULE·I·(j)
A ball has moved only if it leave its original position · · · if it merely oscillate it has not moved · · ·

RÈGLE I (j)
Une balle n'a bougé
que si elle a quitté
sa position primitive
...si elle ne fait
qu'osciller, elle n'a pas bougé...

PAR FOR THE COURSE

Par is the score that a first-class player is expected to get for a hole, allowing two putts on the green. A par 3 hole is one where the green is considered to be within range of a good tee shot; a par 4 hole one where the green is within range of two shots in normal weather conditions; and a par 5 hole one in which the green is considered to be outwith the range of two shots. A par 3 hole (for men) is one that measures 250 yards or less; a par 4 hole one that measures between 251 and 475 yards; and a par 5 hole one that measures over 475 yards. These distances were established several decades ago and still operate today, even though top professionals can often, in normal weather conditions, reach a par 5 hole quite comfortably in two strokes.

BIRDIE, EAGLE, ALBATROSS

When a player returns a score of one-under-par (i.e. a 3 at a par 4 hole) he (or she) is credited with a "birdie". If a player has a score of two-under-par for a hole then that is described as an "eagle" (i.e. a 2 at a par 4 hole, or a 3 at a par 5 hole). If a 2 is scored at a par 5 hole then it is described as an "albatross".

BOGEY

"Bogey" was a term once used in Britain to describe a score that the average club golfer would be expected to get at a hole. The term fell into disuse as par began to be used instead, but was adopted in the United States to describe a score of one-over-par (i.e. a 5 at a par 4 hole) when the officially recognised description in Britain and elsewhere was one-over-par. However since the Second World War, the use of "bogey" to describe one-over-par, or "double bogey" for two-over-par, has become quite commonplace. In 1951 one of the British golf writers who attended the Ryder cup match at Pinehurst, North Carolina wrote: "We deplored the American practice of describing one-over-par as 'bogey' and the way the players said 'I started par, bogey, bogey, birdie... ' but before the visit was over Dai Rees and some of his team mates were 'bogeying' away with the best of them."

EAGLE AT A PAR 3 HOLE

When a player holes his (or her) tee shot at a par 3 hole it is an "eagle", but it is rarely, if ever, referred to as that. It is described as a "hole-in-one" or an "ace".

Does it help you to consciously start the
clubhead straight back?
-Swing Thought No. 21.

MAY

17

18

1951-Rodger Davis, born Sydney, Australia. Winner of more than 20 tournaments and championships worldwide since 1977. Runner-up in Open Championship in 1987.

19

20

21

22

23

1946-David Graham, born Tasmania. Winner of 1981 U.S. Open and of 1979 U.S.P.G.A. Championship.

GOLF WRITERS ASSOCIATION

The Association of Golf Writers was formed in 1938 at the time of a Walker Cup match between the amateurs of the British Isles and the United States at St. Andrews. Its purpose was to obtain an improvement in working conditions for the golfing press, though the late Henry Longhurst, one of the original members, once jocularly remarked that its prime purpose was to persuade railway station masters to have sleepers available (the normal method of travel in those days for golfers and others attending major events) to travel from London to St. Andrews, Muirfield and Carnoustie, all championship venues on Scotland's east coast.

WRITERS' HALL OF FAME

Peter Dobereiner, one of the outstanding British writers on golf during the past two decades, is to be inducted this month, May 1993, into a hall of fame for golf writers established by Jack Nicklaus at the Muirfield Village Golf Club, Dublin, Ohio, annual venue for Nicklaus' own tournament on the U.S.P.G.A. Tour. Previous British golf writers inducted into the hall of fame have been Bernard Darwin, Henry Longhurst, Pat Ward-Thomas, Tom Scott, Leonard Crawley and Percy Huggins.

PROFESSIONAL GOLFERS' ASSOCIATION

The Professional Golfers' Association came into being in 1901 and one of the leading lights in its creation was J.H. Taylor (one of the famous turn-of-the-century Triumvirate) who by then had won the Open Championship three times. It was founded to promote interest in the game; to protect and advance the mutual and trade interests of its members; to hold meetings and tournaments periodically for the encouragement of the younger members; to institute a benevolent fund for the relief of deserving members; to act as an agency for assisting any professional golfer or club maker to obtain employment; and to effect any other objects of a like nature. The present headquarters of the Association are at The Belfry, near Sutton Coldfield, venue for the last two Ryder Cup matches played in Britain.

24

25

26

27

1912-Sam Snead, born Virginia. Winner of Open Championship in 1946. Three times winner of the U.S. Masters and three times winner of the U.S.P.G.A. Championship. Runner-up four times in the U.S. Open. Won world senior professional titles five times. Played for U.S. in seven Ryder Cup matches. At the age of 62 tied for third place in U.S.P.G.A. Championship.

28

29

30

The NEW all in one folding

Hill Billy®
POWERED GOLF TROLLEY

A new concept in powered golf trolleys – the Hill Billy combines the advantages of a conventional pull trolley with the very best of modern engineering, battery technology and advanced manufacturing processes.

We designed our trolley to be tough and reliable. To ensure this, all components have been "over specified", from the award winning one way clutch design to the powerful drive unit and purpose made battery charger.

Battery performance has always been a problem with powered trolleys, with many batteries unable to withstand the strains imposed by the constant charge and discharge. Every Hill Billy is supplied with a purpose made battery from Yuasa, a world leading producer of sealed batteries, along with Yuasa approved design charger. With proper use, this combination makes battery problems a thing of the past.

The Hill Billy powered trolley is manufactured in the UK using British components. It is simplicity itself to handle. Weighing only 14lbs, it requires no assembly but just unfolds with a click in one easy movement.

The care and attention to detail embodied in this innovative design is continued through manufacture and quality control in modern factory conditions to ensure the highest degree of reliability.

Unit 32, Joseph Wilson Ind. Est.,
Whitstable, Kent. CT5 3PS. England.
TEL: 0227 771910
FAX: 0227 772777

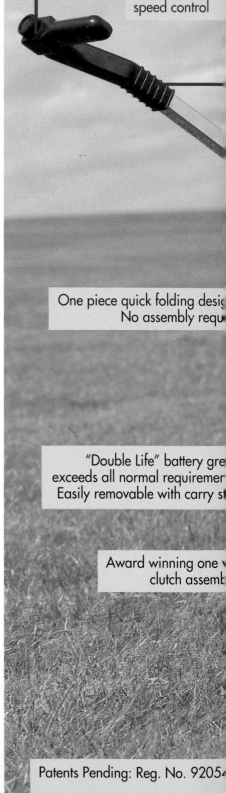

Smooth progres
speed control

One piece quick folding desi
No assembly requ

"Double Life" battery gre
exceeds all normal requiremen
Easily removable with carry s

Award winning one
clutch assemb

Patents Pending: Reg. No. 92054

dle adjustable for
r right hand operators

ce of pull or push operation

Flexible and immensely
strong nylon bag carriers –
Suit all normal bag sizes

Tough long lasting finish to
all components

Hill Billy

Purpose designed heavy duty
maintenance free motor and
sealed drive unit

All major components easily serviceable

COMPACT GOLF COURSES

Golf courses can often be laid out most compactly. The sketch is of a layout of a 9 hole course in Bavaria, at Herzogen Aurach, not far from Nuremberg. The course measures 6090 metres (for 18 holes) for men. Requests on the scorecard to observe the rules of etiquette are printed in German and in English.

BRITAIN'S GOLFING NEEDS

In mid-summer in 1992, the British Institute of Golf Course Architects organised what was described as the first international conference on golf course design, location and environment to be held in the United kingdom, after which the following statement was issued: **"The conference delegates... concluded that the traditional figures used by the Sports Council to gauge the level of provision needed - one course for every 35,000 people - is now seriously out of date and instead called for a new benchmark figure of one course every 25,000 people to be adopted in order to cater for growing demand. At least 1.7 million players** presently play on 1,700 courses, while demand for the game has more than doubled in just 20 years. A speaker informed the conference that, in recession-struck 1990 alone there were over 1,000 applications for golf courses throughout the United Kingdom. William Hillary, senior partner in a firm of chartered surveyors, pointed out that 170 - 200 acres are needed for a typical golf course - more if extensive areas of woodland or amenity land are included - and that the successful application would be more likely to include a new clubhouse of 4,000 - 5,000 square feet; double that for a well located major golf centre with full retailing facilities."

GOLF-CLUB
HERZOGENAURACH E. V.

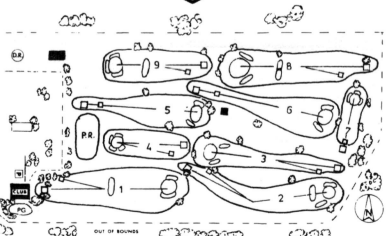

Bitte ausgeschlagene Rasenstücke einsetzen, Bunkerspuren einebnen, Pitchmarken ausbessern, Golfetikette beachten.

Please replace all divots, smooth footprints in traps, repair all ballmarks on green, observe golfing-etiquette.

MAY/JUNE

31

1

2

1953-Craig Stadler, born California. Winner of the 1982 U.S. Masters Tournament. Has
played for the U.S. both as an amateur (Walker Cup) and as a professional (Ryder Cup).
Nicknamed the "walrus" because of his distinctive moustache.

3

1945-Hale Irwin, born Montana. Winner of the U.S. Open in 1974, 1979 and 1990.
Runner-up in Open Championship in 1983. Winner of the World Match-Play
Championship in 1974 and 1975. Played for U.S. in five Ryder Cup matches.

4

5

6

RULE XVI
When ye balls lie within six inches of each other . . . (the distance to be measured from their nearest points.)

RÈGLE XVI
Lorsque les balles
sont à six pouces l'une de l'autre...
(la distance à mesurer
est celle de leurs points
les plus proches).

THE STYMIE

For many years the stymie was a part of match play golf, though the word did not appear in the rules of the game. A player was said to be stymied on the green when he had to putt while his opponent's ball lay on his line to the hole. The player was only allowed to have his opponent's ball lifted while he putted if his ball and that of his opponent lay within six inches of each other. (N.B. This was why score cards for use in club competitions and other events were exactly six inches across so that they could be used, if required, for measuring purposes). If the two balls lay more than six inches apart then the player had to try to negotiate the stymie, either by lofting his own ball over that of his opponent or by trying to play a curling putt round his opponent's ball, by making use of a slope on the green, or the nap of the grass, or by trying to cut his own ball round the obstructing ball. A change made in the *Rules of Golf* in 1951 eliminated the stymie from the game. Prior to 1951 a rule had stated: *"When the balls lie within six inches of each other on the putting green (the distance measured from the nearest points) the ball lying nearer to the hole may, at the option of either the player or the opponent, be lifted, until the other ball is played..."* From 1951 the rule was changed to stipulate that the player, if he considered that his opponent's ball was interfering with his play, could have it lifted.

JOHN BALL'S RECORD IN THE AMATEUR

John Ball set a record for the Amateur Championship which has never been equalled by winning the title eight times. He did so between 1890, the fourth year in which the event was played, and 1912. In addition he was twice a finalist and also appeared in the semi-finals three times. To put it another way - in the thirteen times he reached the semi-finals he went on to win the title eight times and to finish runner-up twice.

7

8

9

10

11

12

1960-Mark Celcavecchia, born Nebraska. Winner of Open Championship in 1989 at Royal Troon after four-hole play-off. Runner-up in 1988 U.S. Masters.

13

STYMIE HAPPENING NO. 1.

One famous championship stymie was unique in that it paved the way to an achievement that has become part of golfing history. It occurred in the 1930 Amateur Championship played over the Old Course at St. Andrews and it involved two great golfers, Cyril Tolley and R.T. (Bobby) Jones. Tolley, twice a winner of the event, was the defending champion. Jones, from Atlanta, Georgia was at the time the undisputed greatest golfer in the world. By the start of 1930 Jones was a multiple winner of three major championships - the Open, the U.S. Open and the U.S. Amateur. But he had never won the Amateur (sometimes called the British Amateur to distinguish it from the American event) though, in fairness, it

Tolley was seven feet away in 3, having mishit his shot to the green and then chipped weakly, whereas Jones was ten feet away in 2 and on the same side of the hole. When Jones putted, his ball stopped two inches short of the cup, right on Tolley's line to the hole - a dead stymie. Jones subsequently said that the hole was completely shut off to anything but a miracle. So Jones won the hole and the match. He was subsequently to say he had always regretted that such a splendid match should have been decided by a stymie, but a stymie was, after all, an accepted part of the game; and Tolley, generous in defeat, considered his weak chip had left him wide open to the possibility of being stymied.

must be pointed out that he had competed in it infrequently. That year the Amateur preceded the U.S. Open, the Open and the U.S. Amateur. By the luck of the draw Jones and Tolley came face to face in an early round. It was hailed by many as the match of the decade, even of the century. Interest was at fever pitch. There was never more than one hole in it. At the 17th, Jones holed from eight feet to stay on level terms. The 18th was also halved and the match went to the 19th. There

Jones went on from that match to win the championship and followed that up by winning the U.S. Open, the Open and the U.S. Amateur once more, all in 1930. No one had ever won those four events in one season and no one has ever come near to doing so. It was an achievement that was described as the Grand Slam and one writer also named it the Impregnable Quadrilateral. After that Jones retired as a championship contender. He was only 28 years of age.

14

1955-Cathy Panton-Lewis, born Stirlingshire. Winner of British women's open amateur championship in 1976. Scottish Sportswoman of the year, 1976. Turned professional 1978. Winner of 14 professional events.

15

16

1941-Tommy Horton, born St. Helens. Played twice in Ryder Cup matches against U.S. Winner of South African Open in 1970.

17

18

19

20

STYMIE HAPPENING NO. 2.

When the 1936 U.S. Amateur Championship was played at Garden City the field included members of the British team that, in the preceding week, had suffered an overwhelming defeat in the Walker Cup match at Pine Valley. One member of the British team, Jack McLean, a Scot who had won his country's national title three times in a row, reached the final, in which he met an American, Johnny Fischer. After having been, at one stage three up, McLean came to the 34th one up. There he looked like going two up with two to play when Fischer fluffed a chip. However Fischer's next shot left the Scot with a dead stymie.

McLean made an effort to loft his ball over his opponent's, and succeeded in doing so, but his ball hit the cup and kicked out. So the hole was halved. Then, after the 35th had been halved in a birdie 4, Fischer squared the match with a 2 at the par 3 last hole and then took the title with another birdie, this time a 3, at the 37th, by holing a putt of ten yards.

STYMIE HAPPENING NO. 3.

When the Scottish Amateur Championship was played in 1947 at Glasgow Gailes, Hamilton ("Hammy") McInally, a one-time miner who had won the two previous championships played on Ayrshire venues (in 1937 and 1939), was twice stymied in a very tight semi-final match which he won after having, each time, successfully lofted his own ball over that of his opponent into the cup. At the end of the match someone complimented him on his dexterity at playing stymies. "Och," he responded, "it's nothing. Just a putt wi' a wedge."

STYMIE HAPPENING NO. 4.

The abolition of the stymie from golf came shortly after the final of the 1951 English Amateur Championship at Hunstanton had been decided by an impossible stymie at the 39th (the third extra hole).

A CADDIE'S DUTIES

Does your address position allow a 90 degree shoulder turn?

-Swing Thought No. 26.

21

22

23

1963-Colin Montgomerie, born Glasgow. Runner-up in 1984 Amateur Championship and winner of 1987 Scottish Amateur Championship before turning professional. Played in 1991 Ryder Cup match. Finished third in 1992 U.S. Open Championship.

24

1931-Billy Casper, born California. Winner of the U.S. Open Championship in 1959 and 1966. Winner of U.S. Masters Tournament in 1970. Played for U.S.A. in eight Ryder Cup matches.

25

26

27

1945-Clive Clark, born Hampshire. Has played against U.S.A. as an amateur (Walker Cup) and professional (Ryder Cup). Now best known as TV commentator.

SUCCESS HASN'T MADE US BIG HEADED.

The Slotline Inertial
HAMMER

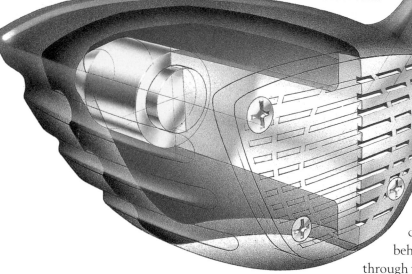

Our original Inertial Putter was one of the best selling putters in history. It proved that all our research and development paid off. So we went back to the drawing board once again to invent a long-hitting driver. But we didn't end up with a big head. You see, most drivers, no matter how big the head, are hollow shells filled with foam.

When hit, they slightly compress, stealing energy and distance from your ball. But ours is made with an aluminum-titanium face that continues directly behind the sweet spot, through the middle of the club-head. Virtually non-compressible, it concentrates more mass directly behind the ball than any hollow driver. The physics work just like a battering ram or a hammer to propel the ball longer. The solid brass backweight puts the bulk of the weight in the back of the club to give it Inertial weighting. Inertial means straighter and ensures a full solid hit from anywhere on the clubface. The Slotline Hammer. We won't let it make us big headed.

For more information,

Telephone JS Golf on 0334 77017

SLOTLINE HAMMER	
232.0 YDS.	○
BIG BERTHA	
215.4 YDS.	○

Average total distance (yds). Clubhead speed 95 mph.

In clubhead vs. clubhead robot testing, the Hammer went 16.6 yards longer and 29.7 percent more accurate than Big Bertha.

The Slotline Hammer comes with a 9.5° or 11° loft. Available in your choice of True Temper Dynamic steel or Aldila Boron Graphite shafts. It is equipped with a soft, leather-wrap pattern tackified grip by Lamkin. Includes a fur-lined head cover.

SLOTLINE
ENGINEERED FOR PERFORMANCE

THEY SAID IT COULDN'T BE DONE.

Nobody believed we could improve upon our famous Inertial Putter. 97% heel-toe weighting gave it the highest resistance to twisting and uncanny accuracy. It quickly became one of the top selling putters in history. But now, our research and development team has made it even better. The new HMI II provides all the advantages of 97% heel-toe weighting, plus a topspin roll that minimizes skidding. So the ball settles into a roll sooner for a stronger, truer line.

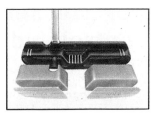

Only Inertial Putters have the patented 3-metal construction. A lightweight aluminum-titanium alloy body, heavy lead inserts and nickel silver caps. It gives the HMI II 97% heel and toe weighting, and the most resistance to twisting of any putter ever made.

Slim-lined designed bore-through hosel is made of polished stainless for ultimate strength and feel.

The Slotline Inertial

HMI II

No matter what the break, your putt will stay more on target. And its stainless steel, bore-through hosel practically eliminates unwanted vibrations for

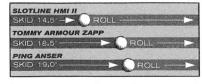

SLOTLINE HMI II		
SKID 14.5" → ○ ROLL		→
TOMMY ARMOUR ZAPP		
SKID 18.5"	○ ROLL	→
PING ANSER		
SKID 19.0"	→ ○ ROLL	→

Distance to start roll on a robot-generated 10-foot putt.

greater feel and touch. The Inertial HMI II Putter. We think it will make believers out of those who said it couldn't be done.

For more information, **Telephone J S Golf on 0334 77017**
Available in offset and straight hosel styles. 34" and 35". Right-hand only.

SLOTLINE
ENGINEERED FOR PERFORMANCE™

OPEN CHAMPIONSHIP

The Open Championship, long recognised as the premier event in the world of golf, began in 1860. It was the brainchild of members of Prestwick Golf Club, a club in Ayrshire, on the west coast of Scotland, which had been in existence for nine years. Initially the Prestwick golfers approached two clubs that had been in existence on the east coast of Scotland - the Honourable Company of Edinburgh Golfers and the Royal and Ancient Golf Club of St. Andrews - with the suggestion that they should join together in staging a 36-hole stroke competition (a rarity in those days) and have venues in

the day, became the permanent possessor of the Challenge Belt with victories in the event in 1868, 1869 and 1870.

The event then went into abeyance for a year during which time the two East of Scotland clubs previously mentioned, agreed to share in the continuing promotion of the event. The three clubs also shared in the purchase of a new trophy, but this time there was no provision for it to become the permanent possession of any competitor who succeeded in winning the championship three times in a row. That trophy is still in use today. When the championship was revived in 1972, Young Tom Morris was again the

winner, making him the only player in the history of the event to win the title four times in a row. For 20 years the event was played by rotation over three courses - Prestwick, Musselburgh (which the Hon. Company shared with other clubs) and the old course at St. Andrews. In

rotation. While the two East of Scotland clubs apparently gave approval to the suggestion, they dragged their heels at the idea they should participate, so the Prestwick Club decided to proceed on its own. In October 1860, eight invited Scottish professionals competed for what was described as the Challenge Belt. When the event was repeated the following year it was announced that it was open to the whole world, and so it has continued to be until this day. The championship was played annually at Prestwick for eleven years until Tom Morris Jnr., one of the outstanding professionals of

1892 the event was staged at Muirfield, which had become the home of the Hon. Company, and that year the championship was also extended to 72 holes. Two years later it was played in England for the first time, at Royal St. George's, Sandwich, Kent, after which the Royal Liverpool Golf Club at Hoylake was brought into the rota, while the Royal Cinque Ports at Deal was also used before the First World War. It was shortly after the war that the Royal and Ancient Golf Club of St. Andrews, by invitation of other clubs, took over the administration and running of the championship, as it still does today.

28

29

30

1952-Dale Hayes, born Pretoria, South Africa. Winner in Europe of Spanish, Swiss, Italian and French Open titles. Was top money winner in Europe in 1975.

1

2

3

4

OPEN BEGAN ON 12 HOLE COURSE

When the Open Championship began at Prestwick the course there measured 12 holes, so the 36 hole event required three rounds. It was only in 1883 that the Prestwick course was redesigned and extended to 18 holes.

PRESTWICK GOLF LINKS

which probably made it in those days, with the equipment available, a par 6. Yet when Young Tom Morris won the title for the third time in 1870 he began his first round with a 3, indicating he probably holed a full third shot. He went on to complete that round in 47, almost certainly the first player ever to return a score less than level 4s.

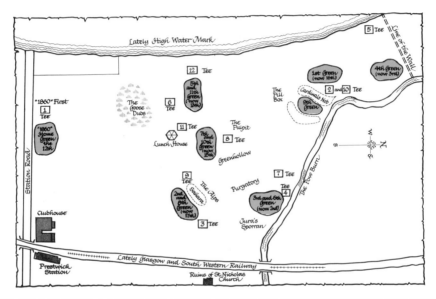

Prestwick Golf Links
based on original layout 1851 to 1882

It was on these Links that
the first Open Championship was held in 1860

BASED ON ORIGINAL LAYOUT 1851 TO 1882. IT WAS ON THESE LINKS THAT THE FIRST OPEN CHAMPIONSHIP WAS HELD IN 1860

The first tee of the original Prestwick course is no longer in use but it is now marked by a cairn that was unveiled in 1977 by Henry Cotton (later Sir Henry Cotton) three-times winner of the Open Championship. That original first hole, used when the Open Championship began, measured 576 yards

THE FIRST HOLE IN ONE IN THE OPEN

The first hole in one in an Open Championship was scored by Young Tom Morris in the first round in 1868 when he achieved the first of his four consecutive victories in the event. He scored it at the 8th, a hole of 166 yards.

FIRST AMATEUR SUCCESSES

The first amateur winner of the Open Championship was John Ball of the Royal Liverpool Golf Club, who gained the title at Prestwick in 1890. Two years later another English amateur, Harold Hilton, became the first player to win the title over 72 holes, at Muirfield.

5

6

7

1944-Tony Jacklin, born Scunthorpe. Winner of the Open Championship in 1969 (first British winner for 18 years). Won U.S. Open in 1970. Third in Open Championship in 1971 and 1972. Played seven times in Ryder Cup matches against the U.S.A., then was captain of the European team for the next four matches, one of which resulted in the first defeat of a U.S.A. team at home.

8

9

10

11

70 BROKEN FOR FIRST TIME

The first player to break 70 for a round in the Open Championship was James Braid in 1904 at Royal St. George's, Sandwich, when he scored 69 in the third round. However it proved to be not enough to win the title for him on that occasion, for Jack White, the Sunningdale professional, scored 69 in the final round to win the event by one stroke, while Braid had to settle for a share of second place with J.H. Taylor who, in the fourth round, established a new championship record of 68.

COTTON'S 65 IN 1934

When Henry Cotton, in the course of winning the Open Championship for the first time at Royal St. George's in 1934, had a new record 18 hole score for the event with a 65 in the second round, the ball manufacturing company whose product he had used during the event, promptly brought out a new ball called the *Dunlop 65*, which continued for many years as probably the best known golf ball in Britain.

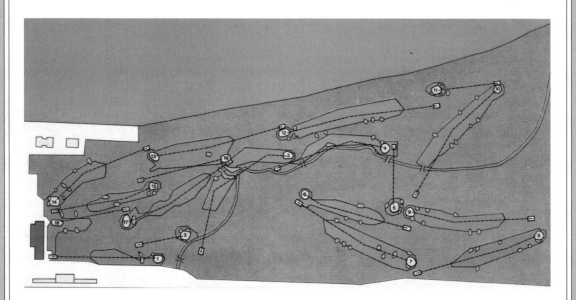

PRESTWICK GOLF COURSE TODAY

RECOIL FROM THE RAILWAY

The present first hole at Prestwick is immediately across a wall from Prestwick railway station and runs parallel to that wall. Once, when it was played as the 19th hole in a club foursome match, the drive and second shot of one foursome pair both bounced back into play from the railway track, the second to finish four feet from the cup, enabling the pair, who had twice been "out of bounds", to win the hole and the match with a birdie 3. It has been said that a player once sliced his tee shot at the first hole over the wall into a passing goods train, for his ball to finish up in Glasgow!

RECORD SCORING IN THE OPEN

The 65 scored by Henry Cotton in the 1934 Open Championship remained the one round record for the event until 1977 when Mark Hayes returned a 63 at Turnberry. Since then three other players have also scored a 63 in the championship - Isao Aoki at Muirfield in 1980, Greg Norman in 1986 (when he won the event) and Jodie Mudd at Royal Birkdale in 1991.

BEN HOGAN'S "THREE IN ONE" YEAR

Ben Hogan of America competed only once in the Open Championship - at Carnoustie in 1953 - and won, by four strokes. Earlier that year he had also won the U.S. Masters and the U.S. Open, making him the first player to win all three of those titles in the same year. To date no one has managed to match that feat.

Do you see the ball throughout the backswing?
-Swing Thought No. 29.

JULY

12

13

1937-Charles Coody, born Texas. Winner of U.S. Masters in 1971.
Subsequently won two 1973 events in Britain.

14

15

16

17

1955-Garth McGimpsey, born 1955. Winner of
Amateur Championship 1985. Has played in
three Walker Cup matches against U.S.A.

18

1957- Nick Faldo, born Welwyn Garden City.
Winner of Open Championship in 1987, 1990
and 1992. Winner of U.S. Masters Tournament
in 1989 and 1990.

STRUCK BY LIGHTNING

On the first qualifying day of the 1936 Open Championship a violent thunderstorm and torrential rain in the early afternoon wiped out the day's play at Hoylake and the auxiliary qualifying course at Wallasey. A news agency writer, who was telephoning his story to London when lightning struck telephone lines outside the press tent, was thrown violently backwards from his bench seat when the electrical discharge travelled to his receiver. His colleague at Hoylake subsequently interviewed him on what it was like to be struck by lightning at the Open Championship.

LAST OPEN AT PRESTWICK

The Open Championship was played for the last time at Prestwick in 1925. The increasing spectator interest in championship golf made it clear on that occasion that the layout of the Prestwick course, with the loop of the last four holes sandwiched between other parts of the course, did not lend itself to large-scale crowd control.

A FAMOUS HAZARD

Prestwick Golf Course's best known hazard is the Cardinal Bunker, a vast expanse of sand which stretches across the present third fairway and which was also a hazard in the original 12 hole layout. The bunker has a sleepered face.

THE ORIGINAL TWELVE

The original twelve holes on which the Open Championship began were:

- 1st   Back of Cardinal   578 yards
- 2nd   Alps   385 yards
- 3rd   Tunnel (Red)   167 yards
- 4th   Wall   448 yards
- 5th   Sea Headrig   440 yards
- 6th   Tunnel (White)   314 yards
- 7th   Green Hollow   144 yards
- 8th   Station   166 yards
- 9th   Burn   395 yards
- 10th   Lunch House   213 yards
- 11th   Short   132 yards
- 12th   Home   417 yards

THREE IN A ROW

Only one player has won the Open Championship three times in a row since it was extended to be a 72 hole event in 1892. That is Peter Thomson of Australia who won the title in 1954 (at Hoylake), in 1955 (at St. Andrews) and in 1956 (at Royal Birkdale). Thomson subsequently went on to win the event twice more.

ROYAL CAPTAIN

A former captain of Prestwick Golf Club was the late Duke of Windsor, when he was Prince of Wales.

THE CARDINAL BUNKER

19

20

21

1930-Gene Littler, born California. Winner of U.S. Open Championship in 1961. Seven times in U.S. team in Ryder Cup matches. Runner-up 1970 in U.S. Masters and in 1977 U.S.P.G.A. Championship. In 1953 won the U.S. Amateur title and played for U.S. in Walker Cup.

22

23

1933-Doug Sanders, born Georgia. Best remembered for missing a shortish last green putt that would have made him Open champion in 1970. He then lost 18-hole play-off for title to Jack Nicklaus. Had also been runner-up to Nicklaus in 1966.

24

25

14 DIFFERENT VENUES

There have been 121 Open Championships to date. They have been played on fourteen different courses, as follows:

- ❒ Prestwick — 24
- ❒ St. Andrews — 24
- ❒ Muirfield — 14
- ❒ Royal St. George's — 11
- ❒ Hoylake — 10
- ❒ Royal Lytham St. Annes — 8
- ❒ Royal Birkdale — 7
- ❒ Musselburgh — 6
- ❒ Royal Troon — 6
- ❒ Carnoustie — 5
- ❒ Royal Cinque Ports — 2
- ❒ Turnberry — 2
- ❒ Royal Portrush — 1
- ❒ Prince's — 1

FORMAT CHANGES IN THE OPEN

For many years, from the mid-20s, the Open Championship was a five day affair, with all the field competing on the first two days in a qualifying competition over the championship venue and an auxiliary course, after which the championship proper began on the Wednesday and ended with the final two rounds on the Friday. This arrangement of a Friday finish, which also applied to sponsored 72 hole professional tournaments, was to enable the professional competitors, who in those days, were basically club professionals, to return to their clubs to be on duty for their members on Saturdays and Sundays. In 1963 qualifying exemptions were introduced for the first time, and in 1966 the event was extended from three days to four (one round per day), with a Saturday finish. As entries for the event increased, more and more qualifying courses were used, followed by two stage qualifying regional events (from which some players were exempt) and final qualifying.

COMMUNAL DINING TABLE

An unusual feature of the clubhouse of Prestwick Golf Club is a communal dining table for the use of members and their guests. A similar communal dining table is to be found at the *Burning Tree Country Club* just outside Washington, U.S.A.

PRESENT DAY VENUES FOR THE OPEN

There are seven golf courses now in regular use as venues for the Open Championship. They are the *St. Andrews Old Course*, *Muirfield* (home of the Honourable Company of Edinburgh Golfers), *Royal Troon* and *Turnberry*, all in Scotland, and *Royal St. George's*, *Royal Birkdale* (Southport) and *Royal Lytham and St. Annes*, all in England.

The clubhouse of Prestwick Golf Club today houses mementoes of the early years of the Open Championship, including the first score cards ever used in golf. These can be seen in a special display by visitors to the club.

It has been said that "hitting from the top" is a common fault.

-Swing Thought No. 31.

JULY/AUGUST

26

1957-Wayne Grady, born Queensland, Australia. Winner of U.S.P.G.A. Championship in 1990. Tied for first place in the 1989 Open Championship but beaten in the play-off.

27

28

29

1916-Max Faulkner, born Bexhill, Sussex. Winner of Open Championship in 1951, at Royal Portrush. Played five Ryder Cup matches against the U.S.A.

30

31

1

THE BOOKS OF DAYS SERIES
from
THE EDINBURGH PUBLISHING COMPANY LIMITED

You're over half way through 1993 and if you have enjoyed this book so far you might wish to know that there are two other Books of Days available - **The Whisky Connoisseur's Book of Days** and **The Gardener's Book of Days**.

These two titles have received as wide a laudatory acclaim as **The Golfer's Book of Days** -

The Whisky Connoisseur's Book of Days by John Lamond
"This book will appeal to those who thirst for accurate and unusual knowledge on the Scotch Whisky industry. With many amusing anecdotes, you'll find that, like a good malt, you'll want to dip into it frequently."

- Richard Paterson, Master Blender, Whyte & Mackay Group PLC.

The Gardener's Book of Days by Faith and Geoffrey Whiten
"Gardens and Gardening offer adventure, romance and fun and that's just part of it. If you find it hard to believe then this charming book will surprise you."

- Roy Lancaster

The Books of Days series will continue with new editions each year and each edition will contain different information of interest and concern to the reader, adding substance to an encyclopaedia of facts, fables, feats and folklore. The unique reference value of the material deserves a place on any bookshelf when the work of the daybook is done.

New Titles in the Books of Days series
The Edinburgh Publishing Company Limited is proud to announce the publication of two further titles in the series for 1994:-

The Traveller's Book of Days
Step back in time to a wonderful world of travel through the ages, up to the present day and even into the future! Indulge in a feast of fascinating facts, fables and folklore from the rich traditions of travel and (whilst perhaps travelling to your destination in a modern airliner, cruise ship or train) enjoy the writings and muse upon the lovely colour and black and white etchings, engravings, sketches and watercolours contained in this book.

A Bride's Book of Days
Getting married? Do you know someone who is? Then this must be the perfect present for that perfect bride. A beautiful collection of beautiful brides, amusing bridegrooms, wonderful weddings - and - the not so wonderful. A superb collection of fascinating facts, fables and folklore from the rich traditions of weddings and brides reaching back to bygone eras. And, like all the titles in **The Books of Days** series, beautifully produced with lovely colour and black and white etchings, engravings, sketches and watercolours. Without doubt **A Bride's Book of Days** will prove the perfect present to recall the most important day in every woman's life.

To be published October 1993.

THE
WHISKY
CONNOISSEUR'S
BOOK *of* DAYS

**Facts, Fables and Folklore
from the World of Whisky**

JOHN LAMOND

Published with The Scotch Whisky Association

The joy of the books is in the quality ot their layout and production, in the quality of their contents and in the quantity of their contents - you can dip into them time and time again and not read the same thing twice.

THE
GOLFER'S
BOOK *of* DAYS

**Facts, Feats and Folklore
from the World of Golf**

PERCY HUGGINS

Published with The Professional Golfers' Association

THE
GARDENER'S
BOOK *of* DAYS

**Facts, Fables and Folklore
from the World of Gardening**

FAITH and GEOFFREY WHITEN

Published with The Garden Centre Association

Remember, there are completely new editions of the above three titles for 1994!

and, for 1993:-

The Traveller's Book of Days

A Bride's Book of Days

To order or for further information contact your local bookshop. In case of difficulty contact The Edinburgh Publishing Company Limited. Telephone 03585 399

THE FIRST ELEVEN

The first eleven championships played at Prestwick were won as follows:

1860	Willie Park, Musselburgh	174
1861	Old Tom Morris, Prestwick	163
1862	Old Tom Morris, Prestwick	163
1863	Willie Park, Musselburgh	168
1864	Old Tom Morris, Prestwick	167
1865	Andrew Srath, St. Andrews	162
1866	Willie Park, Musselburgh	169
1867	Old Tom Morris, St. Andrews	170
1868	Young Tom Morris, St. Andrews	157
1869	Young Tom Morris, St. Andrews	154
1870	Young Tom Morris, St. Andrews	149

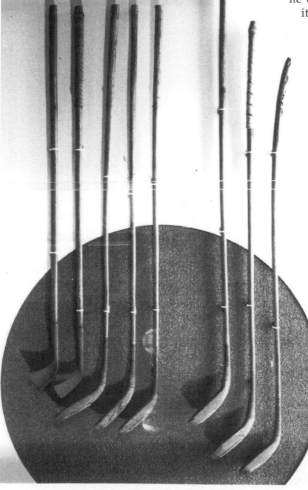

THE POSTAGE STAMP

The par 3 8th hole on the Royal Troon championship course is known as the *Postage Stamp* because of its tiny green, guarded by bunkers. In the 1950 Open Championship played there a German amateur, Herman Tissies, scored a 15 at that hole, being in all three bunkers as he "ping-ponged" back and forth, taking five strokes in one of them, and finally taking three putts. When that championship was played, an experimental rule was in operation, making the reduced penalty for an unplayable ball loss of distance only. In one round Roberto de Vicenzo of the Argentine, who finished runner-up to Bobby Locke (South Africa), found his ball in one of the bunkers but lying in such a way that a shot to the green would have been hazardous. So he declared the ball "unplayable" (though it could have been played) went back to the tee, played another shot from there close to the cup, and holed the short putt to give him a par 3. The experimental rule was subsequently scrapped. When another Open Championship was played at Troon in 1973, the veteran American professional Gene Sarazen (the 1932 winner of the title) competed to mark the 50th anniversary of his appearance in the event (also at Troon) and in the first round, scored a hole in one at the Postage Stamp, and almost repeated the feat in the second round.

BRITISH WINNERS OF THE OPEN

Since the end of the First World War only twelve British players have won the Open Championship, and only two of them have won it more than once. The late *Sir Henry Cotton* won it three times, in *1934, 1937* and *1948* and *Nick Faldo* has won it three times, in *1987, 1990 and 1992*. In addition three British-born professionals who emigrated to the United States won the title between 1921 and 1931.

It has been said that downswing recoil begins at the feet.

-Swing Thought No. 32.

AUGUST

2

3

4

5

6

1922-Doug Ford, born Connecticut. Winner of U.S. Masters in 1957; and of the U.S.P.G.A. Championship in 1955. Represented the U.S. four times in Ryder Cup matches.

7

1952-Eamonn Darcy, born Delgany. Has played in four Ryder Cup matches against the U.S.A. Has won tournaments in Europe, Africa and New Zealand.

8

FEATHER BALLS

The feather ball was the standard one in use until the 1850s. The ball flew well in dry condition, but in wet weather it became soft and lost its shape. It was easily split into pieces, especially if mis-hit with an iron club. The longest drive with a feather ball was 361 yards by Samuel Messieux at St. Andrews in the 1830s. Old feather balls can fetch high prices at auction and the four balls illustrated here, all dating from about 1840, at a Christie's auction in Glasgow in 1989, each sold, respectively from left to right, for £2,640, £2,090, £2,090 and £2,310 each.

The making of first-class feather balls was almost a science. The leather was of untanned bull's hide, two round pieces for the end and a strip for the middle were cut to suit the weight wanted. These were properly shaped, after being sufficiently softened, firmly sewn together (with a waxed linen thread) - a small hole being of course left, through which the feathers might be afterwards inserted. But, before stuffing, it was through this little hole that the leather itself had to be turned outside in, so that the seams should be inside. The skin was then placed in cup-shaped stand, the worker having the feathers (from the breast of a goose or chicken) in an apron in front of him, and the actual stuffing done with a crutch-handled steel rod (known as a brogue), which the maker placed under his arm. And very hard work, I may add, it was. Thereafter the aperture was closed and firmly sewed up: and this outside seam was the only one visible.

-Reminiscences of Golf and Golfers,
H. Thomas Peter, 1890

TABLEAU IN THE BRITISH GOLF/MUSEUM OF ALLAN ROBERTSON MAKING A FEATHER BALL

Do you keep the hands passive, starting down, as some advise?

-Thought Swing No. 33.

AUGUST

9

10

11

12

13

1912-Ben Hogan, born Dublin, Texas. Winner of Open Championship in 1953; of U.S. Open in 1948, 1950, 1951 and 1953; of U.S. Masters in 1951 and 1953; and of U.S.P.G.A. Championship in 1946 and 1948. Is one of only four player who have won all of those four events and is the only player who has won three of them - Open, U.S. Open and U.S. Masters - in one year (1953).

14

15

In 1848 a new type of golf ball appeared that was to have a gradual but profound impact on the game. This ball was formed from a solid piece of gutta percha, a black rubber-like substance that came from the juice of the Palaquium genus of trees. A sheet of material was cut into pieces and softened in hot water. It was wound into a ball, heated again and pressed until it was as solid as possible. It was then dropped into cold water to harden.

The early balls did not fly as far as featheries. It was soon discovered that they went further when marked or nicked. Ballmakers then began hammering onto the balls and later this was done with moulds and then machines. At best a gutta percha ball only went as far as a feather ball, having relatively little bounce or carry after hitting the ground. However, it was a much more durable ball and was considerably cheaper.

In the 1870s, other materials were mixed in with the gutta percha to produce what was known as the composition or gutty ball. It is almost impossible to discern the difference in the balls, so the names gutta percha and gutty are usually considered to be interchangeable.

-British Golf Museum

GUTTY BALL MOULD

Where the SCOTO GOLF BALLS
ARE MADE. ARE MADE.

Makers of the famous ORDERS are NOW being BOOKED for the
CRAIGPARK SCOTO GOLF
GOLF . .
BALLS . . BALLS

CRAIGPARK WORKS.
THE CRAIGPARK COMPANY, LIMITED,
Telegraph Wire and Cable Manufacturers, Townmill Road, Dennistoun, Glasgow.
LONDON ADDRESS . . 190, UPPER THAMES STREET, E.C.

BALL ADVERTISEMENT, 1891

·GUARANTEED·
·MADE·FROM·
NEW MATERIAL

EVERY SILVERTOWN GOLF BALL HAS NAME EMBOSSED ON IT

THE SILVERTOWN GOLF BALLS

THOROUGHLY SEASONED

WORKS, SILVERTOWN, ESSEX, LONDON, E. & PERSAN BEAUMONT, FRANCE.
WAREHOUSES 100 & 106, CANNON ST. LONDON, E.C. & 97, BOULEVARD SEBASTOPOL, PARIS.

BOX OF GUTTY BALLS, C.1890

16

17

18

19

1958-Gordon Brand, Jnr., born Fife. Was British youth champion in 1979. Has played against the U.S.A. as an amateur (Walker Cup) and as a professional (Ryder Cup). 1948-Christy O'Connor, Jnr., born Galway. Finished third in Open Championship in 1985. Played in Ryder Cup matches against the U.S. in 1975 and 1989.

20

21

22

LEADERS NOW GO OUT LAST

It is now established practice that in the Open Championship and in 72 hole professional tournaments and other events, the leaders after 36 holes, and again after 54 holes, will tee-off last. This came about to suit the television coverage of golf. Prior to that, because of order of play draws made prior to an event, the halfway leader could tee-off at any point in the third round. For instance, when Henry Cotton won the Open Championship for the third time at Muirfield in 1948, when the final two rounds were still played in one day, he was not only the halfway leader but teed-off first in the third and fourth rounds. This happened because the Royal and Ancient used to make three draws prior to an Open Championship. The first was for the order of play in the two qualifying rounds (on a Monday and Tuesday) in which all those entered had to compete; the second for the order of play for the first two rounds of the championship proper; and the third for the order of play in the final two rounds. The names of all players entered for the event went into the draw. At the completion of the qualifying rounds the names of those who had failed to qualify were deleted from the second draw and also, of course, from the third draw. After 36 holes of the championship had been played, the names of those who had failed to qualify for the final two rounds were also deleted. In 1948 this left Cotton's name at the top of the draw for the final 36 holes.

When television coverage began it was quickly realised that it was not practical to have all the leading contenders for the title scattered through the order of play draw for the final stages of the event.

EARLY TV COVERAGE

In the early days of live coverage of golf on television one of the first events projected on TV screens was an Open Championship at St. Andrews where, at the far end of the Old Course, there is a mound from which play on the 6th, 7th, 8th, 9th, 10th, 11th and 12th holes can be viewed. It was an ideal spot on which to place a TV camera, or so it was thought. This coverage provided viewers with a great deal of interesting play but, of course, did not inform them of how players had completed their round. So it was realised that, while coverage of the play round the Old Course loop, as it is called, was interesting, it was the score at the end of the round that mattered. So a camera was installed to cover play at the 18th and programme changes were made to permit end-of-round coverage.

O n June 1st and 2nd, 1939, Reg Whitcombe and the young South African, Bobby Locke, played a £1,000 Challenge match at Coombe Hill Golf Club. What made this event unusual was that it was the first golf match in Britain to be televised.

FIRST TELEVISED GOLF MATCH, 1939

23

1929-Peter Thomson, born Melbourne, Australia. Five times winner of the Open Championship in 1954-55-56-58 and 65. Only player to have won the title three times in a row since the championship became a 72-hole event. Numerous other championship and tournament achievements, including the 1954 P.G.A. match-play championship. An honorary member of the R. and A.

24

1953-Sam Torrance, born Largs, Ayrshire. Has played in six Ryder Cup matches against the U.S.A. and has made numerous other international appearances. Has won Scottish Professional Championship three times.

25

26

27

1957-Bernhard Langer, born Germany. Winner of U.S, Masters in 1985. Runner-up in the Open Championship in 1981 and 1984. Has been in six Ryder Cup match teams against U.S.A. Has won open titles in Germany, France, Holland, Austria, Italy, Spain and Ireland.

28

29

THE BEST KEPT SECRET IN GOLF!

RE - GRIP WITH AVON NEXUS AND DISCOVER JUST HOW GOOD A GRIP CAN BE.

AVON - THE PREMIUM QUALITY, HIGH - PERFORMANCE, LONG LIFE GRIP. SIMPLY YEARS AHEAD.

THE FIRST RULES OF GOLF

The first rules of golf were drafted in 1744 by the Gentlemen Golfers of Edinburgh (subsequently to be known as the Honourable Company of Edinburgh Golfers) after they had persuaded the City of Edinburgh to present a silver club for annual competition over the five holes of the Links of Leith. These rules have been the basis of all rules subsequently drafted. There were 13 in all:

1. You must tee your Ball within one club's length of the hole.

2. Your tee must be upon the ground.

3. You are not to change the ball you strike off the tee.

4. You are not to remove Stones, Bones or any Break Club, for the sake of playing your Ball, except upon the Fair Green, and that only within a Club's length of your Ball.

5. If your Ball come among watter or any wattery filth, you are at liberty to take your Ball and bringing it behind the hazard and teeing it, you may play it with any club and allow your adversary a Stroke, for so getting out your Ball.

6. If your balls be found anywhere touching one another you are to lift the first ball, till you play the last.

7. At Holing, you are to play your Ball honestly for the Hole, and not play upon your adversary's ball, not lying in your way to the Hole.

8. If you should lose your Ball, by its being taken up, or any other way, you are to go back to the Spot where you struck last, and drop another Ball, and allow your adversary a Stroke for the misfortune.

9. No man Holing his Ball is to be allowed to mark his way to the Hole with his Club or anything else.

10. If a Ball be stopp'd by any person, Horse, Dog or anything else, the Ball so stopp'd must be play'd where it lyes.

11. If you draw your Club, in order to Strike, and proceed so far in the Stroke, as to be bringing down your Club; If then your Club shall break, in any way, it is to Accounted a Stroke.

12. He whose Ball lyes farthest from the Hole is obliged to play first.

13. Neither Trench, Ditch or Dyke, made for the preservation of the Links, nor the Scholar's Holes or the Soldier's Lines, shall be accounted a Hazard. But the Ball is to be taken out and Tee'd and play'd with any Iron Club.

N.B. Golf was originally only a match play game; hence the wording of some of the first rules. Ten years after these rules had been drafted by the Edinburgh golfers they were adopted by the golfers of St. Andrews when in 1754 they formed the club, the Royal and Ancient Golf Club of St. Andrews . There was one change made in Rule 5, though whether this change was made by the St. Andrews golfers or had already been made by the Edinburgh golfers, is not clear. The rule, originally said that when a ball was taken out of "watter" or "wattery filth", the procedure was "bringing it behind the hazard and teeing it". The change subsequently made stated that the procedure was "throwing it behind the hazard 6 yards at least, you may play it with any club..." No reference, it will be noted, to teeing up the ball.

VIII. EARLY RULES OF GOLF

Extract from the first Minute Book of "The Society of St. Andrews Golfers" on its formation in 1754.

30

31

1942-Isao Aoki, born Japan. Won the World Match-Play Championship at Wentworth in 1978 and the European Open in 1983.

1

2

3

4

1949-Tom Watson, born Kansas, Missouri. Winner five times of Open Championship; twice winner of U.S. Masters; and winner of 1982 U.S. Open.

5

RULE XXXIII
A player shall not
ask for advice
from anyone but
his··caddie··nor
shall he willingly
be otherwise
advised *in any
way whatever*, ·

RÈGLE XXXIII
Un joueur ne demandera d'avis
de nul autre que de son... caddie...
n'acceptera non plus volontairement
de conseil de quiconque
en aucune façon...

"HAMMY'S" ARMY IN AYRSHIRE

"Arnie's Army" (enthusiastic followers of Arnold Palmer) has been a familiar part of the American golf scene during the past three decades. More than half a century ago there was a Scottish amateur who had his own "army". He was Hamilton McInally, known as "Hammy", who hailed from a mining village in Ayrshire and who had been for a time a miner before becoming a shipyard worker in the nearby town of Irvine. "Hammy's" army first materialised when he competed in the 1937 Scottish Amateur Championship at Barassie, an Ayrshire course, and reached the closing stages of that event. By the time he played against the defending champion, E.D. Hamilton, in the semi-finals, his supporters were out in force and made no secret of where their sympathies lay. "Hammy" won the title that year and captured it again two years later when the championship returned to Ayrshire, at Prestwick. He lost his title in 1946 but captured it again the following year when the championship was once more back in Ayrshire, at Glasgow Gailes. Each time "Hammy" had enthusiastic followers. In 1953, when the championship was on another Ayrshire course, Western Gailes, and the ex-champion once more got to the closing stages, the "army" reappeared. When "Hammy's" semi-final match was in progress against the eventual winner, David Blair, two of his supporters met up behind one of the greens and greeted each other. Then one looked in astonishment at the admission badge in the jacket lapel of his acquaintance and exclaimed, "Why, you didn't pay to get in, did you?"

Apart from being a fine and successful golfer "Hammy" McInally was also quite a character. On one occasion he was playing for Scotland in the amateur home internationals at Hoylake and, in his singles match, was several holes up at the turn. The non-playing team captain, noting this, made a mental note that that was one point in the bag and went off to watch some of the other play. Later on he was astonished to see the match in which "Hammy" was engaged going down the 17th. "What happened?" he asked. "Och," said "Hammy", "I showed him (meaning his opponent) what he was doing wrong and now we are having a real fine game."

SEPTEMBER

6

7

1923-Louise Suggs, born in Georgia. Winner of British women's amateur championship in 1948; winner of U.S. women's amateur championship in 1947; subsequently turned professional and has more than 50 major tournament and championship wins.

8

9

10

1929-Arnold Palmer, born Pennsylvania. Winner of Open Championship 1961 and 1962; winner of U.S. Open 1960; winner of U.S. Masters 1958, 1960, 1962 and 1964.
1951-Bill Rogers, born Texas. Winner of Open Championship 1981; winner of Suntory World Match-Play Championship 1979.

11

1942-Tom Weiskopf, born Ohio. Open Champion 1973.

12

"HAMMY" AND THE ADMIRAL

The stories about "Hammy" McInally are legion. He was in the Royal Navy during the war as an able seaman and at one stage, stationed somewhere in the east coast of England, he made his way in bell-bottom trousers, and with clubs slung over his shoulder, to a nearby golf course. In the clubhouse was a semi-retired English admiral, so anxious for a game, that he invited the able seaman to join him. "Hammy" was more than willing. The admiral, in his ignorance, thinking that anyone in bell-bottom trousers could not be much of a player, suggested that he give "Hammy" a stroke a hole. "Hammy", who was of course, the reigning Scottish champion, agreed! It must have been quite a match.

WHEN "HAMMY" PLAYED EWING

"Hammy" McInally always enjoyed a flutter. If there were two flies on a window he'd wager which would reach the top of the window first. In 1949, when all but two places in the team to play the United States in a Walker Cup match were announced ahead of the Amateur Championship, which was played in Portmarnoc, "Hammy" was not selected and Irishman Cecil Ewing was, when many thought it should have been the other way round. As luck would have it McInally and Ewing were drawn to play each other in the championship - and Irishmen are as eager to have a flutter as McInally was. The Scot won on the last green and his progress back to the clubhouse was punctuated by stops as one Irishman after another approached to hand over to him his winnings.

"HAMMY" IN THE AMATEUR CHAMPIONSHIP

"Hammy" McInally always enjoyed a noggin. In the first post war Amateur Championship at Birkdale in 1946, he would have a favourite Scottish tipple of an evening - whisky and beer (a half and a half pint). But, on the Thursday evening, when he was into the quarter-finals, a crony tried to persuade him to be teetotal that night, saying that he had as much chance as anyone left in the field to win the title. "Hammy" demurred, then compromised. He would only drink beer that evening, which he did. The following morning he was narrowly beaten. As he then walked into the clubhouse bar for a tipple he declared, "That's the last time I'll ever go into training."

SEPTEMBER

13

14

15

16

1953-Jerry Pate, born Georgia. Winner of U.S. Open 1976.
Winner of U.S. Amateur Championship 1974.

17

1955-Scott Simpson, born in California. Winner of U.S. open
1987; runner-up (after play-off) in 1991.

18

19

THE GATE TO GOLF

A few weeks before the outbreak of the First World War there had been a surprise winner of the French Open Championship. He was J. Douglas Edgar, a professional from Northumberland who, for years, had competed without success or impact, in the Open Championship and other events. Then, shortly after Harry Vardon had won the 1914 Open Championship for a record sixth time, Edgar made this breakthrough, with Vardon and the other great professionals of the day also in the field. He finished six strokes ahead of Vardon and eight strokes ahead of J.H. Taylor. Then war broke out and Edgar was unable to cash in, as it were, on his achievement. Following military service he headed for the United States, obtained a position in Atlanta, Georgia and soon began to make his presence felt. Indeed he won the first post-war Canadian Open with an aggregate of 278, a record for such an event in those days and by what was a record margin of 17 strokes, even with the great players like Walter Hagen and the developing Bobby Jones in the field. Edgar retained the title the following year but only after a triple tie and an 18 hole play-off. Then in 1921, he died violently in a street in Atlanta. It was thought he might have been a hit-and-run victim. But there was also a strong suspicion that he had been murdered, though no one was ever charged with that offence. Shortly before his death he had published a book called *The Gate to Golf*. It was a description of the "in-to-out" swing, something completely new in those days. The book was sold with a gadget that enabled golfers to practise "swinging through the gate". It was a discovery about the golf swing that had preceded his victory in the French Open and his subsequent successes on the other side of the Atlantic. After his death many tributes were paid to his golfing skill and his swing

FROM THE FRONT COVER OF "THE GATE TO GOLF"

knowledge. He was credited with being the father of the modern American swing, while one great golfer who subsequently won both the Open and the U.S. Open Championships said that he had learned from many fine players, but most of all from Edgar. Alas, Edgar did not live to gain financial rewards from the publication of his book. He was 37 when he died.

SEPTEMBER

20

1955-Jose Rivero, born in Spain. Tournament winner in Europe since 1984. Twice played in Ryder Cup.

21

22

23

1958-Larry Mize, born in Georgia. Winner of 1987 U.S. Masters, beating Seve Ballesteros and Greg Norman in sudden death play-off.

24

25

26

1934-Neil Coles, born London. Played eight times in Ryder Cup matches in 18-year period. British Seniors Open Champion 1987.

F or more than a decade Pro-Golf Worldwide's unique personalised Custom Fitting Service has been used by professionals on the World Tour.

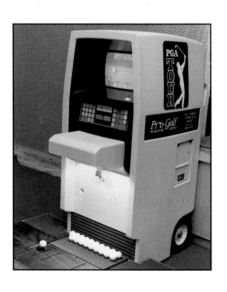

Whether you are an amateur or a professional, the improvement is dramatic.

The average handicap reduction by our clients is 25 %.

Using the latest "state of the art" computer technology, we will customise clubs to suit your particular strength, build and ability.

THE IMPORTANCE OF POSTURE

Robert Russell was an Ulster-born manufacturing confectioner based in south London. He was not of a particularly athletic build and he never shone at any sport. In his mid-40s he was introduced to golf, took lessons from two highly regarded teaching professionals, decided that neither could appreciate the problems of the late beginner, then applied himself to such a degree that, by the age of 49, he was able to play to what he himself described as a "scratchy handicap of eight". One day, watching some famous professionals in an exhibition match, he felt he had spotted what was needed to give him the chance to become a really good golfer; namely, a better posture at address. A visit to a physiotherapist in Harley Street persuaded him that he was on the right lines and, from Loughborough College of Physical Education, he obtained exercises to straighten the base of his spine. Under expert supervision he did these exercises for two months without touching a golf club. Then, when he returned to the game, he immediately began to play scratch golf, at the age of 50. Years later he was persuaded, reluctantly, to write about his own ideas on the golf swing for a magazine. There

ROBERT RUSSELL ON HIS 80TH BIRTHDAY

followed a lengthy association with that magazine, *Golf Monthly*, for which he wrote under the pen name of Mr. X. During that association three Mr. X. books were also published, the first going into a number of reprints and also being published in the United States. As a golfer Russell continued to return scores in the mid-70s even when close to the age of 80. He was proof that, in golf, it is never too late to learn.

MATCH STICK MEN SHOWING ANGLES AS FEATURED IN GOLF MONTHLY

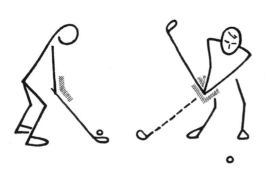
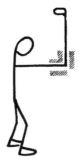

27

28

1935-Bruce Crampton, born in Sydney, Australia. Settled in U.S.A. and
became first non-American to win more than $1,000,000 in prize money.

29

30

1

1939-George Archer, born in California. Winner of U.S. Masters 1969. Winner of 12
events on U.S. Tour. Now distinguished competitor in senior professional events.

2

3

1959-Fred Couples, born Seattle. Winner of
U.S. Master in 1992. Third in Open in 1992.

RECORD PRICE FOR A GOLF CLUB

The auctioning of golf antiques and other memorabilia is now big business. Each year the well known firms of *Christie's*, *Philips* and *Sotheby's* hold such auctions during the week of the Open Championship. Collectors from all over the world attend, including members of a long established Collectors Society in the U.S.A. The 1992 sales produced something special - a golf club that went for £92,400 at the Sotheby's auction, beating the previous record price for a golf club by nearly £40,000. The club, a rake iron, made either in the late 17th or early 18th century, was recently discovered in a garden shed in Edinburgh. The bidding ended at £84,000, but the buyer also had to pay a 10% premium which is levied by the auctioneers at their sales. The club was bought by Titus Kendall, who was bidding on behalf of Jamie Ortiz-Patino, a billionaire who owns the Valderrama club on Spain's Costa del Sol, where he is planning to set up a golfing museum. He spent a total of £180,000 at the auction for pieces to be exhibited in his museum. The seller of the club was a 56-year old carpenter, who wished to remain anonymous. He had been given the club by his father and had kept it wrapped in a cloth soaked with linseed oil.

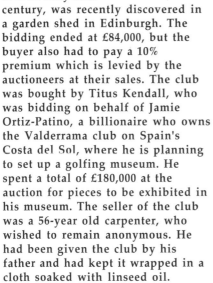

The rubber core ball, where elastic was wound around the core of the ball and then covered in gutta percha, was patented in the U.S.A. in 1899 by Coburn Haskell and Bertram Work, the latter of the B.F. Goodrich Rubber Company in Ohio. Two years later J. Gammeter, also of Goodrich, invented the first automatic golf ball winding machine, which allowed the whole ball-making process to be mechanised. The Haskell first appeared in Britain in 1901 and immediately caused a controversy. The ball, which travelled further, especially when hit with an iron club, and was more lively on the greens, was also very expensive. In 1902 the best gutta percha ball cost 1 shilling whereas the new rubber core cost 3 shillings. The following year the advertised price dropped to 2 shillings.

- British Golf Museum

In 1992, during the week of the Open Championship, the medal won by Fred Herd in the 1898 U.S. Open was auctioned by Sotheby's for £15,000. Four years later Fred's brother Sandy (Alex) won the Open Championship. Sandy won with the then revolutionary *Haskell* wound ball, whereupon other competitors who had been using the gutty ball switched to the new ball.

Do you have a feeling that your best shots are
achieved without any conscious effort?
                              -Swing Thought No. 41.

OCTOBER

4

5

6

7

8

1963-Laura Davis, born in Coventry. Winner of 1986 British women's open championship; winner of 1987 U.S. women's open championship. As an amateur reached Curtis Cup status.

9

1916-John Panton, born Pitlochry. Eight times Scottish professional champion (once tied). Three times played in Ryder Cup. Top British player in 1956 Open Championship.

10

WORLD'S BEST IN THE MID-19TH CENTURY

In the middle of the 19th century a St. Andrews ball-maker (of featheries), Allan Robertson, had the reputation of being the finest golfer in the world, who, it was said, was never beaten in a challenge match on level terms. It was indeed regrettable that Robertson did not get the opportunity to prove himself in the Open Championship when that event began in 1860. He died two years previously, at the age of 43.

THE TOM MORRIS JUNIOR TRAGEDY

After Tom Morris Junior won the Open Championship four times in a row in 1872, he finished joint third in 1873 and runner-up in 1874. The following year, when he and his father were playing a challenge match in North Berwick against the Park brothers, he received news at the end of the match, that his wife was seriously ill following a confinement. A yacht was put at his service to enable him to get back speedily to St. Andrews, but another telegram arrived to tell of his young wife's death. Young Tom never recovered from this tragic loss and on Christmas Day that year he died, at the age of 24.

MEDAL FOR YOUNG TOM

When Young Tom Morris won the Open Championship for the third time in a row in 1870, to make him the permanent holder of the Challenge Belt (which was the trophy for the event) a special medal to mark the occasion was commissioned by Prestwick Golf Club. The medal said: *"Winner of the Championship Belt at Prestwick 3 years in succession, viz: - 23rd Sept 1868 at 154 strokes, 16th do., 1869 at 157, and 15th do., 1870 at 149."*

OCTOBER

11

12

13

14

15

16

17

THE TRIUMVIRATE

For 21 years the Open Championship was dominated by three players who became known as the Triumvirate. They were Harry Vardon, who hailed from the Channel Islands, J.H. Taylor, who came from north Devon and James Braid, a Scot who was originally a joiner in Fife. Between them, in those 21 years, they won the Open Championship a total of 16 times. Vardon won the title six times, and Taylor and Braid five times each. No one has yet equalled Vardon's record of six wins in the event, and only two players - Peter Thomson of Australia and Tom Watson of the United States - have equalled the Braid/Taylor tally of five victories. Taylor was the first of the Triumvirate to capture the title, in 1894, and repeated that success the following year. Vardon had his first win the following year, and had two more successes, and Taylor one more, before Braid recorded his first Open win in 1901. The Scot then had a spell of four wins in six years to make him, in 1910,

the five-times winner of the championship. He was joined on that mark by Vardon the following year, and by Taylor in 1913, so that they were on level terms competing in the 1914 Open Championship, to discover if one of them could become the first six-times winner. Vardon proved to be that player. Not long afterwards the Great War began and, when the championship was resumed in 1920, a new generation of players had taken over.

THE WHITCOMBE BROTHERS

During the 1920s and 1930s three brothers featured prominently in the championship and tournament scene in Britain. They were the Whitcombe brothers - Ernest, Charles and Reginald. Charles won the P.G.A. Match-Play Championship (which in those days was the most important event in Britain after the Open Championship) in 1928 and 1930, his older brother Ernest having won the same event in 1924. Charles played in the first six Ryder Cup matches between 1927 and 1937 and captained the Great Britain team three times. Ernest played in three of those six matches and on one occasion partnered brother Charles in the foursomes. Reginald, the youngest of the brother, began to make his presence felt when he reached the semi-finals of the match-play championship in 1934 and 1935. In the Open Championship, during the period when players from across the Atlantic dominated the event, Ernest was once runner-up while Charles had fourth, fifth and sixth place finishes. It was left to young Reginald to succeed where the older brothers had failed, by taking the Open title during the gale-lashed final day of the 1938 championship at Royal St. George's, Sandwich. It was said that Reginald's flat-footed swing, a feature of the action of all the brothers, contributed to his success in the gale. Ironically Reginald never played in a Ryder Cup match. He was chosen to play in 1939 in America but war broke out before that match could be played.

18

19

20

21

1926-Bob Rosburg, born California. Winner of U.S.P.G.A.
Championship in 1959. Twice runner-up in U.S. Open.

22

23

24

1960-Ian Baker-Finch, born in Queensland,
Australia. Winner of 1991 Open
Championship.

TRANQUILITY IS THE SECRET

"When Braid, Taylor and I were much-of-a-muchness, and playing together frequently in exhibition matches, we were always desperately keen to beat one another. Golf is not a game at which one dare slacken, even in a friendly game. Only, if you play rounds every day at high tension for two or three weeks before the championship, you are very likely to lose your zest through sheer staleness. Somebody has said that golf is 'nine-tenths mental'. The estimate is not far wrong. For that reason, training which involves compliance with regulations that are irksome is apt to be a bane rather than a blessing to your game. For this game you need, above all things, to be in a tranquil frame of mind."

-Harry Vardon,
Golf Monthly, 1921

Vardon's swing... is the very poetry of golf, full of concentrated ease and grace, of supple energy so applied as never to be obvious. It exemplifies the art of concealing the art. His play is the embodiment of smooth, even, machine-like accuracy...

-Magazine article, 1904

In playing on the green,
Though rivalry be keen,
With courtesy forever fill your role;
Antagonists may gain,
Yet kindly you'll refrain
From talking till the
      ball
      is
      in
      the
      hole...

Though warm may be the day,
And hot the game you play,
Yet you should keep as cool as Arctic pole;
Let others fret and fume,
The calmest air assume
And keep it till the
      ball
      is
      in
      the
      hole

-*Golf* from *The Elgin Courant and Courier,*
Tuesday December 24th 1895

Do you finish completion of swing facing your target?

-Swing Thought No. 44.

25

26

27

28

1953-Mark James, born in Manchester. Five times played in Ryder Cup. English amateur champion in 1974. Walker Cup international, 1975.

29

30

31

When the crowds bunch and gather at the front, it's irksome.

—

If his rainwear did, it would irk some more.

h, the pressures of fame. Especially if you're one everiano Ballesteros.

Everywhere you go, the owds are sure to be there. And occasionally, even if u're as good as Seve, you ind up where the crowds ready are - some distance f the fairway!

Seve has such a range of scape' shots, you'd think it as Houdini with his hands n the golf clubs.

And of course, it's the very rilliance of Seve's recovery nots that makes him so exciting to watch.

The trouble is, no matter how uch Seve may have grown sed to the crowds, they can ill prove a huge distraction.

And distractions, large or mall, are the last thing a olfer needs.

Seve copes with the crowds by joking with them: "I know you are nervous, but so am I!" is typical.

But you can't swap jokes with your rainwear.

And Seve, in particular, has always had to take his rainwear very seriously indeed.

Seve grew up playing golf in Pedreña, where it rains buckets.

In 1982, he was more than pleased to discover Sunderland.

He played in the Suntory World Matchplay Championship at Wentworth.

For the first time in his life, he could stay dry in the rain, drive freely and putt quietly.

Because he was wearing Sunderlands he'd had the wisdom to buy himself.

Naturally, he won.

Ever since then, Seve and Sunderland have been virtually inseparable.

Making the perfect golf rainsuit is no easy task.

The main problem lies in accommodating the stress points: wrist, elbow, shoulder and half-back.

There has to be enough fabric to allow for a full, free swing and follow-through. But not so little that the jacket 'rides up', exposing the golfer's back and side to the elements.

Too much fabric again, and it will bunch and gather at the front, hampering your putting stroke maddeningly.

Sunderland have long been equipped to cope with these problems masterfully.

We've been tailors through 4 generations now, for well over 80 years.

All our suits are made by hand. Only the best fabrics are used. (We test dozens of new fabrics a year.)

Every Sunderland suit is guaranteed absolutely waterproof. (The deluge of water that pounds our suits during our notorious 'shower' test makes the rainfall in Pedreña seem like a spot of light drizzle.)

Our head of production is John McLaren, ex-pattern cutter at Burberrys, bearers of a Royal Seal for rainwear.

And we have a panel of well over 20 Scottish professional golfers to call on for the most practical advice.

All this is excellent news for Seve. Because now, thanks to Sunderland, all that's left to irk him are the crowds.

SUNDERLAND
of Scotland

WE REIGN WHEN IT POURS

 GORE-TEX® fabrics   SUNDERLAND SPORTSWEAR LIMITED P.O. BOX 14, GLASGOW G2 1ER SCOTLAND *(FACSIMILE: 041-552 8518)* TELEPHONE: 041-552 3261/4
The official rainwear of the Professional Golfers Association, Ladies Professional Golf Association and The Women Professional Golfers' European Tour.

CARTOONIST ROY ULLYETT

Outstanding as a cartoonist of the golfing scene (and of other sports, particularly cricket) for more than four decades, has been Roy Ullyett of the *Daily Express*. It is an indication of the way in which his work has been appreciated that he has produced the cartoon covers for the dinner menus at functions of the *Professional Golfers' Association* and of the *Association of Golf Writers,* of which he has been an honorary member since 1948. The accompanying cartoon, from the 1980 P.G.A. dinner menu, featured extrovert Brian Barnes, who had begun opting on occasion for wearing shorts.

On very short shots (i.e. chips) do you avoid
trying to "scoop" the ball...
-Swing Thought No. 45.

NOVEMBER

1

1935-Gary Player, born in Johannesburg, South Africa. One of only four players to have won the Open Championship (three times), the U.S. Open (once), the U.S. Masters (three times), and the U.S.P.G.A. Championship (twice). Undoubtedly the most successful player not born in Britain or the U.S.A. in the history of the game.

2

3

4

5

6

7

HE "CAUGHT" HIMSELF OUT!

When John Ball won the Amateur Championship for the eighth and last, time, it was at Westward Ho! in 1912. His opponent in the final was Abe Mitchell, who subsequently turned professional and was described in later years as the finest golfer never to win the Open Championship. The final ended at the 38th hole and it was recorded that it did so when Mitchell caught his ball as it rose almost perpendicularly from a ditch from which he attempted a recovery shot.

A SHOT THROUGH A HAT

Freddie Tait, winner of the Amateur Championship in 1896 and 1898, died at the height of his golfing prowess in the Boer War. The story was told of his having, at St. Andrews, driven a golf ball through a man's hat and so had to pay the owner five shillings to purchase a new one. Afterwards Tait grumbled to veteran professional Tom Morris about the cost to him of that particular shot. The professional responded, "Mr. Tait, you ought to be glad it was only a new hat you had to buy, and not an oak coffin."

THE SCHENECTADY PUTTER

The first foreigner to win the Amateur Championship was W.J. Travis, a native of Australia who had become a naturalised American citizen. His success was 1904. He won with a Schenectady putter, which was centre-shafted, never before seen in Britain. The authorities promptly declared centre-shafted putters illegal and they remained so for many years.

A SONG TO GOLF BALLS

Though gouf be of our games most rare,
Yet, truth to speak, the wear and tear
Of balls were felt to be severe
　　And source of great vexation;

When Gourlay's balls cost half a crown,
And Allan's not a farthing down,
The feck o's wad been harried soon
　　In this era of taxation.

Right fain were we to be content
Wi' used up balls new lick't wi' paint,
That ill concealed baith scar and rent -
　　Balls scarcely fit for younkers.

And though our best wi' them we tried,
And nicely every club applied,
They whirred, and fuffed, and dooked, and shied
　　And sklentit into bunkers.

Ye're keen and certain at a putt -
Nae weet your sides e'er opens up -
And though for years your ribs they whup,
　　Ye'll never moutt a feather!

Hail, gutta percha, precious gum!
　　　　　　　　　　　-Dr. Graham, 1848

...and remember to leave it to the club's loft to lift the ball?

-Swing Thought No. 46.

NOVEMBER

8

1921-Jack Fleck, born in Iowa. Won the 1955 U.S. Open, beating Ben Hogan in an 18-hole play-off for the title, so baulking Hogan of a record fifth win in the event.

9

10

11

1951-Fuzzy Zoeller, born in Indiana. Winner of the U.S. Open in 1984 and winner of the U.S. Masters in 1979.

12

13

14

WAR RULES (1939-45)

The following rules were drafted out by the secretary of St. Mellons Golf Club during the early part of the war when Luftwaffe bombers frequently attacked targets in Britain:

1. Players are asked to collect bomb and shell splinters from the fairways to save these causing damage to the mowers.

2. In competitions, during gunfire, or while the bombs are falling, players may take cover without penalty for ceasing play.

3. The positions of known delayed-action bombs are marked by red and white flags placed at reasonably, but not guaranteed, safe distances from the bombs.

4. Shell and/or bomb splinters on the greens may be removed without penalty. On the fairways or in bunkers within a club's length of a ball that may be moved without penalty, and no penalty shall be incurred if a ball is thereby caused to move accidentally.

5. A ball moved by enemy action may be replaced as near as possible to where it lay, or if lost or destroyed a ball may be dropped not nearer the hole without penalty.

6. A ball lying in any crater may be lifted and dropped not nearer the hole, preserving the line to the hole, without penalty.

7. A player whose stroke is affected by the simultaneous explosion of a bomb or shell, or by machine gun fire, may play another ball from the same place. Penalty one stroke.

These war time rules were adopted by many other clubs, particularly in the midlands and south of England.

BEWARE of MANTRAPS AND SPRING GUNS

· RULE IX ·

Any loose
impediment··
··may be
removed····

RÈGLE IX
Toute chose mobile...
...peut être déplacée...

Expert greenside bunker shot players
recommend an open stance for such shots.
-Swing Thought No. 47.

NOVEMBER

15

16

17

18

1936-Brian Huggett, born Porthcawl, South Wales. Played six times against the U.S.A. in Ryder Cup matches. Runner-up in Open Championship in 1965.

19

20

1929-Don January, born in Texas. Winner of U.S.P.G.A. Championship in 1967.

21

FALDO AND NICKLAUS

Nick Faldo has now won five major titles in the space of six seasons (three Open Championships and two U.S. Masters titles). In addition he tied for first place with Curtis Strange in the 1988 U.S. Open but was beaten in an 18 hole play-off. By comparison Jack Nicklaus had six wins in those three events in six seasons, beginning with his first victory in the U.S. Open in 1926. So it could be said that Faldo came within a stroke of tying the Nicklaus achievement.

NICKLAUS'S 31 APPEARANCES

When Jack Nicklaus competed in the 1992 Open Championship at Muirfield it was his 31st consecutive appearance in the event which he has won three times, the last occasion being in 1978. No other American has ever come anywhere near approaching this tally.

FAMOUS MIDDLE NAME

The full name of Larry Mize, the American professional who won the 1987 U.S. Masters Tournament, by holing a long chip in a sudden death play-off, is Larry Hogan Mize. No guess who it was his parents admired.

HOGAN AT CARNOUSTIE'S 6TH

After two rounds of practice at Carnoustie for the 1953 Open Championship Ben Hogan, making another circuit of the course, hit a drive at the par 5 sixth hole. Reaching his ball he then sent his caddie up to the green with the following instructions, "I am going to hit three long iron shots from here to the green, one to hit the ground on the left front of the green, the next at centre front and the third at right front. I want you to tell me exactly how each ball bounces, and in what direction, after it touches the ground." The caddie went up to the green and Hogan then hit the three long iron shots exactly as he had predicted.

Christy O'Connor's ten appearances in Ryder Cup matches constitutes a record for the event.

SARAZEN AND CARNOUSTIE' 6TH

In 1937 Gene Sarazen, a winner of both the Open and U.S. Open Championships, said in an interview, "I believe the sixth hole at Carnoustie, played against the wind, is the nearest approach to a perfect par five in the world."

HOGAN AND THE SMALLER BALL

When Ben Hogan came to Scotland in 1953 to prepare for the Open Championship at Carnoustie the 1.62in. ball (the smaller ball) was still the legal ball for use in Britain, but it was illegal in the United States where the 1.68in (or larger) ball was standard. It was generally accepted that the smaller ball could be hit further than the larger ball. After his third day of practice at Carnoustie Hogan was asked if he would be using the 1.62in. ball or the 1.68in ball in the championship. Hogan replied, "It's got to be the British ball. You can hit it out of sight."

Sometimes a half-top hit with wedge is the shot from a thick fringe.

-Swing Thought No. 48.

NOVEMBER

22

23

24

25

1923-Art Wall, born in Pennsylvania. Winner of U.S. Masters Tournament in 1959. Was leading money winner on the U.S. Tour in 1959.

26

27

28

McGIBBON'S
PREMIUM SCOTCH WHISKY

The McGibbon's Golf Range was created on the strength of the natural links between the royal and ancient game of golf and Scotch Whisky, in their traditional homeland of Scotland.

The success story of the McGibbon's Ceramic Decanters has been built not only on the fine Scotch Whiskies but also on the ever-increasing popularity of the Game of Golf, reflected in the packaging of these most Special and Reserve blends

SPECIAL RESERVE - GOLF CLUB DECANTER

The Decanter is a ceramic replica of a golf driver, exact in every detail right down to the four brass screws on the club face. The piece, produced in one of Scotland's most notable potteries, contains the **Special Reserve Blend** - a real sipping whisky for the 19th hole. **The Golf Club Miniature,** which is gift boxed and contains the same excellent **Special Reserve Blend**, is available as a gift or for collectors and those who seek the charm of the **Golf Club Decanter**, but in a smaller capacity.

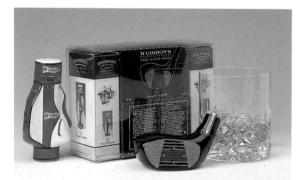

PREMIUM RESERVE - Numbered Edition - GOLF BAG DECANTER

Attention to detail is often ignored within today's commercial parameters, but this replica of a modern golf bag is perfect in every detail including zips, buckles and pouches. Its exquisitely smooth **Premium Reserve Blend** with an unusually high Highland Malt content is certain to delight the discerning connoisseur.

The individual numbering of each decanter confers a degree of exclusivity upon the purchaser. Furthermore, the Master Blender sees the numbering of each decanter as his individual seal of approval, and as a method of quality control.

A cork base to avoid table scratches is applied and the Bag is available in British Racing Green and Pillar Box Red, attractively packed.

McGIBBON'S

"SCOTCH FOR SWINGERS"

The **Golf Bag Miniature** contains the same **Premium Reserve Blend** and the company logo embossed in wax on the base of each decanter, ensuring a perfect seal. Like the larger version, the miniature is attractively gift boxed and available in both colours.

The McGibbon's golf decanters are filled close by some of the world's famous Golf Courses, produced unhurriedly, they should be savoured at an equally leisurely pace.

Douglas McGibbon

Available from: Douglas McGibbon & Co Ltd

Douglas House, 18 Lynedoch Crescent, Glasgow G3 6EQ Tel: 041 333 9242 Fax: 041 333 9245

Golf Rules in Brief is a pocket-sized publication useful to carry on the course as a reminder, if required. It is put out by Royal Insurance, with the approval of the Royal and Ancient Golf Club of St. Andrews, and is obtainable free at any Royal Insurance Office.

PRIZE MONEY FOR THE OPEN

The prize money in the 121st Open Championship played at Muirfield in July 1992 was a record £950,000, an increase of £50,000 on the previous year. The winner, Nick Faldo, received £95,000 and any player who completed the four rounds of the championship received at least £3,200.

RECORD ENTRY FOR MUIRFIELD

The entry for the 1992 Open Championship at Muirfield was 1666, a record for that venue. It compares with the entry of 66 when the championship was first played at Muirfield in 1892.

SPECIAL JUNIOR CLUB AT MUIRFIELD

At the 1992 Open Championship at Muirfield an innovation by the R. and A. and Schweppes was the provision of a tent for the sole use of juniors and their parents, to serve as a junior club at which all Schweppes drinks were sold to juniors at special prices.

LARGEST IN THE WORLD

The exhibition tent at the 1992 Open Championship at Muirfield set new standards as the largest outdoor golf exhibition in the world. It contained 223 stands in an area of 58,000 square feet.

TRYING OUT CLUBS AT THE OPEN

A new feature in the exhibition tent at the 1992 Open Championship at Muirfield was the setting up of a club trial area at one end of the tent. There were 14 practice areas, one for each of the 14 major club manufacturers, who were among the exhibitors. There was also, outside the tent, a practice putting green where, for a small charge, putters supplied by manufacturers could be tried out, with proceeds going to the *Trefoil Centre for the Disabled* in Edinburgh.

29

30

1

1939-Lee Trevino, born in Dallas, Texas. Winner of Open Championship in 1971 and 1972; winner of U.S. Open Championship in 1968 and 1971; winner of U.S.P.G.A. Championship in 1974 and 1984. Played for U.S. in six Ryder Cup matches.

2

3

4

5

1949-Lanny Wadkins, born in Virginia. Winner of U.S. Amateur Championship in 1970. Has been runner-up in the U.S. Open and winner in 1977 of the U.S.P.G.A. Championship.

WHEN ALL CLUBS HAD NAMES

In days gone by golf clubs had names. But, since the end of the Second World War, there has been a swing to clubs being given numbers instead of names, though golfers will still speak of their driver, now also the No. 1. wood and their wedge, in addition to of course, the putter. A full set today will usually consist of three woods (though the heads are now often of metal) ten irons and a putter. The following shows how clubs used to be named:

- ○ No. 1. Wood   Driver
- ○ No. 2. Wood   Brassie
- ○ No. 3. Wood   Spoon
- ○ No. 1. Iron   Driving Iron
- ○ No. 2. Iron   Mid-Iron
- ○ No. 3. Iron   Mid-Mashie
- ○ No. 4. Iron   Mashie Iron
- ○ No. 5. Iron   Mashie
- ○ No. 6. Iron   Spade Mashie
- ○ No. 7. Iron   Mashie Niblick
- ○ No. 8. Iron   Pitching Niblick
- ○ No. 9. Iron   Niblick
- ○ No. 10. Iron   Wedge (modern)

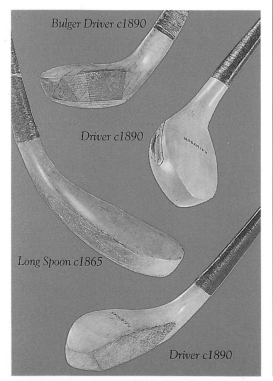

Bulger Driver c1890

Driver c1890

Long Spoon c1865

Driver c1890

LIMIT OF 14 CLUBS

The maximum number of clubs that a player can carry is 14. This rule was introduced shortly before the Second World War, a reaction to the fact that some players from the United States competing in the Open and Amateur Championships were having their caddies carry massive sized bags that contained anything up to two dozen or more, clubs. Prior to the introduction of this rule many golfers, particularly at club level, played quite happily and effectively, with only 8, 9 or 10 clubs. But the manufacturers of clubs were quick to give the impression that a golfer was ill-equipped unless he was carrying 14 clubs.

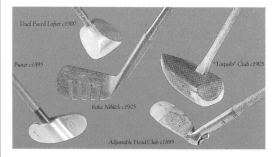

Dual Faced Lofter c1900

Putter c1895

"Torpedo" Club c1905

Rake Niblick 1905

Adjustable Head Club c1895

DESCRIPTION OF A PLAY CLUB

When Sir W.G. Simpson wrote a book called *The Art of Golf* published in 1887, it included the following : *"Nearly everyone carries a play club, an instrument consisting of many parts. It has no legs, but a shaft instead. It has however, a toe. Its toe is at the end of its face, close to its nose, which is not on its face. Although it has no body it has a sole. It has a neck, a head... (Clubs) always have a whipping, but this has nothing to do directly with striking the ball. There is little expression on the face of a club. It is usually wooden; sometimes however, it has a leather face. Clubs, without being clothed, occasionally have lead buttons, but never have any button-holes. Heads are some black, some yellow, but colour is not due to any racial difference. From this description it will be easy to understand, without a diagram, what a club is like."*

6

7

8

9

1949-Tom Kite, born Texas. Winner of the U.S. Open Championship in 1992.
Leading all-time money winner on U.S. Tour. Has played in six Ryder Cup matches.
1933-Orville Moody, born in Oklahoma. Winner of the U.S. Open in 1969.

10

11

12

FALDO'S THREE OPEN WINS

When Nick Faldo won the 121st Open Championship at Muirfield in July 1992, he became the first British player since the late Henry Cotton to win the title three times. Indeed Cotton and Faldo are the only two British players who have won the title more than once since the days of the Triumvirate, which ended in 1914. An interesting point of comparison is that Faldo had his three wins in six consecutive championships, while Cotton had his three wins in nine consecutive championships. On his way to winning the title for the third time Faldo, with opening rounds of 66 and 64, established a new record low aggregate of 130 for the first 36 holes of the championship. The previous best was 132, first achieved by Cotton at Royal St. George's, Sandwich in 1934, when he won the title for the first time and subsequently matched by Faldo himself and Greg Norman (Australia) at St. Andrews in 1990. When Faldo added a third round of 69 for an aggregate of 199, he equalled the lowest total for the first 54 holes of the event, achieved by himself at St. Andrews in 1990. His success in 1992 made him only the second player to have won the championship twice at Muirfield, the first player being Scot James Braid (of the famous Triumvirate) in 1901 and 1906.

THE COCK O' THE GREEN

So thoroughly did he enter into the spirit of the game that every other consideration seemed obliterated for the time. "By the la' Harry," or "By gracious, this won't go for nothing!" he would exclaim involuntarily, as he endeavoured to ply his club with scientific skill; and when victory chanced to crown his exertions, he used to give way to his joy for a second or two by dancing round the golf-hole.

-From, *Golf: A Royal and Ancient Game*, **Robert Clark**, 1873

By the la' Harry Thus shall not go for Nothing

126

13

14

15

16

17

1952-Mickey Walker, born in Yorkshire. As an amateur won the British women's open amateur championship in 1971 and 1972. As a professional was runner-up in the British women's open championship in 1979. Was a founder member of the European professional tour for women.

18

19

NEW RECORD IN U.S. OPEN

At the third hole of the third round in the 1992 U.S. Open Championship at Pebble Beach, California, Gil Morgan established a new record for the event when he took his score to 10 under par. No player had ever previously been as many as ten strokes under par at any stage in the event. Morgan then proceeded to take his score to 12 under par with birdies at the 6th and 7th holes of the round, to establish yet another record and to give him a commanding lead over the rest of the field. Then strokes began to slip away and he finished in a tie for 13th place, eight strokes behind winner Tom Kite.

EIGHT HAVE NOW SCORED 60

The record score for a single round in a European P.G.A. Tour event is 60. It has been made eight times. Two of these seven were achieved in the 1992 Monte Carlo Open - Darren Clarke (23) of Ireland in the second round and Johan Rystrom of Sweden in the fourth round. Players who had previously 60 on the European Tour were Baldovino Dassu of Italy in the 1971 Swiss Open, David Llewellyn of Wales in the 1988 Biarritz Open and Ian Woosnam in the 1990 Monte Carlo Open. A week after the double in the 1992 Monte Carlo Open another 60 was scored, this time in the Bell's Scottish Open in the second round at Gleneagles Hotel King's Course, by English professional Paul Curry. Then Jamie Spence had a final round of 60 to win the Canon European Masters in Switzerland.

Ian Woosnam won the 1992 Monte Carlo Open in early July and it was his third consecutive win in the event. It was the first such achievement by a professional in an important 72 hole stroke event in Europe since Peter Thomson (Australia) won the Open Championship in 1954, 1955 and 1956.

OPENING ROUNDS OF 64

When Raymond Floyd and Steve Pate, both of the U.S.A., both scored 64 in the first round of the 1992 Open Championship at Muirfield they equalled the lowest score ever recorded for the first round of the event. Previous players to begin with the same score were Craig Stadler in 1983, Christy O' Connor Jnr. in 1985 and Rodger Davis in 1987.

RULE XXXI
If a ball lie in fog
... only so much
thereof shall be
touched as will
enable ye player
to find his ball ·

RÈGLE XXXI
Si une balle se trouve en brouillard...
Ne sera touché que ce qui permettra
au joueur de trouver sa balle.

DECEMBER

20

21
1920-Kel Nagle, born in Sydney, Australia. Won the 1960 Open Championship (the Centenary Open, at St. Andrews). Runner-up in the U.S. Open in 1965 after a first-place tie and 18-hole play-off. Is an honorary member of the R. and A. 1924-Christy O'Connor, born in Galway. Played against U.S.A. in ten Ryder Cup matches. Runner-up in open Championship in 1965. In 1958 teamed with Harry Bradshaw to win the Canada Cup, now World Cup.

22

23

24

25

26

A HUNDRED GOLFERS

Air - *"A Hundred Pipers"*

Wi' a hundred golfers an' a', an' a', -
The club, the cleek, an' the ba', the ba',
O, Bruntsfield Links look braw, look braw, -
Wi' a hundred golfers an' a', an' a'.

The *Burgess* are auldest of a', of a' -
Wi' Roberston, Martin, an' Shaw, an' Shaw -
Fresh laurels they gain, which weel they maintain,
Though their vet'rans are wearin' awa', awa'.
The *Brunstfield* comes next in the raw, the raw,
Wi' the *Burgess* they've oft a fracas, fracas;
To add to their honours most gallantly Chambers
Frae St. Andrews a prize brought awa', awa'.

Wi' a hundred golfers an' a', an' a' -
The club, the cleek, an' the ba', the ba',
O, Bruntsfield Links look braw, look braw, -
Wi' a hundred golfers an' a'. an' a'.

We trust that one of the preceding swing thoughts has helped you to trim at least one stroke (hopefully, several) from your handicap.

-Swing Thought No. 53.

DEC/JAN

27

28

1946-Hubert Green, born in Alabama. Winner of U.S. Open in 1977; winner of U.S.P.G.A. Championship in 1985; runner-up in U.S. Masters in 1979. Three times a Ryder Cup player.

29

30

31

1

2

1993

January

S	M	T	W	T	F	S
					1	2
3	4	5	6	7	8	9
10	11	12	13	14	15	16
17	18	19	20	21	22	23
24	25	26	27	28	29	30
31						

February

S	M	T	W	T	F	S
	1	2	3	4	5	6
7	8	9	10	11	12	13
14	15	16	17	18	19	20
21	22	23	24	25	26	27
28						

March

S	M	T	W	T	F	S
	1	2	3	4	5	6
7	8	9	10	11	12	13
14	15	16	17	18	19	20
21	22	23	24	25	26	27
28	29	30	31			

April

S	M	T	W	T	F	S
				1	2	3
4	5	6	7	8	9	10
11	12	13	14	15	16	17
18	19	20	21	22	23	24
25	26	27	28	29	30	

May

S	M	T	W	T	F	S
						1
2	3	4	5	6	7	8
9	10	11	12	13	14	15
16	17	18	19	20	21	22
23	24	25	26	27	28	29
30	31					

June

S	M	T	W	T	F	S
		1	2	3	4	5
6	7	8	9	10	11	12
13	14	15	16	17	18	19
20	21	22	23	24	25	26
27	28	29	30			

July

S	M	T	W	T	F	S
				1	2	3
4	5	6	7	8	9	10
11	12	13	14	15	16	17
18	19	20	21	22	23	24
25	26	27	28	29	30	31

August

S	M	T	W	T	F	S
1	2	3	4	5	6	7
8	9	10	11	12	13	14
15	16	17	18	19	20	21
22	23	24	25	26	27	28
29	30	31				

September

S	M	T	W	T	F	S
			1	2	3	4
5	6	7	8	9	10	11
12	13	14	15	16	17	18
19	20	21	22	23	24	25
26	27	28	29	30		

October

S	M	T	W	T	F	S
					1	2
3	4	5	6	7	8	9
10	11	12	13	14	15	16
17	18	19	20	21	22	23
24	25	26	27	28	29	30
31						

November

S	M	T	W	T	F	S
	1	2	3	4	5	6
7	8	9	10	11	12	13
14	15	16	17	18	19	20
21	22	23	24	25	26	27
28	29	30				

December

S	M	T	W	T	F	S
			1	2	3	4
5	6	7	8	9	10	11
12	13	14	15	16	17	18
19	20	21	22	23	24	25
26	27	28	29	30	31	

1992

January
S	M	T	W	T	F	S
			1	2	3	4
5	6	7	8	9	10	11
12	13	14	15	16	17	18
19	20	21	22	23	24	25
26	27	28	29	30	31	

February
S	M	T	W	T	F	S
						1
2	3	4	5	6	7	8
9	10	11	12	13	14	15
16	17	18	19	20	21	22
23	24	25	26	27	28	29

March
S	M	T	W	T	F	S
1	2	3	4	5	6	7
8	9	10	11	12	13	14
15	16	17	18	19	20	21
22	23	24	25	26	27	28
29	30	31				

April
S	M	T	W	T	F	S
			1	2	3	4
5	6	7	8	9	10	11
12	13	14	15	16	17	18
19	20	21	22	23	24	25
26	27	28	29	30		

May
S	M	T	W	T	F	S
					1	2
3	4	5	6	7	8	9
10	11	12	13	14	15	16
17	18	19	20	21	22	23
24	25	26	27	28	29	30
31						

June
S	M	T	W	T	F	S
	1	2	3	4	5	6
7	8	9	10	11	12	13
14	15	16	17	18	19	20
21	22	23	24	25	26	27
28	29	30				

July
S	M	T	W	T	F	S
			1	2	3	4
5	6	7	8	9	10	11
12	13	14	15	16	17	18
19	20	21	22	23	24	25
26	27	28	29	30	31	

August
S	M	T	W	T	F	S
						1
2	3	4	5	6	7	8
9	10	11	12	13	14	15
16	17	18	19	20	21	22
23	24	25	26	27	28	29
30	31					

September
S	M	T	W	T	F	S
		1	2	3	4	5
6	7	8	9	10	11	12
13	14	15	16	17	18	19
20	21	22	23	24	25	26
27	28	29	30			

October
S	M	T	W	T	F	S
				1	2	3
4	5	6	7	8	9	10
11	12	13	14	15	16	17
18	19	20	21	22	23	24
25	26	27	28	29	30	31

November
S	M	T	W	T	F	S
1	2	3	4	5	6	7
8	9	10	11	12	13	14
15	16	17	18	19	20	21
22	23	24	25	26	27	28
29	30					

December
S	M	T	W	T	F	S
		1	2	3	4	5
6	7	8	9	10	11	12
13	14	15	16	17	18	19
20	21	22	23	24	25	26
27	28	29	30	31		

1994

January
S	M	T	W	T	F	S
						1
2	3	4	5	6	7	8
9	10	11	12	13	14	15
16	17	18	19	20	21	22
23	24	25	26	27	28	29
30	31					

February
S	M	T	W	T	F	S
		1	2	3	4	5
6	7	8	9	10	11	12
13	14	15	16	17	18	19
20	21	22	23	24	25	26
27	28					

March
S	M	T	W	T	F	S
		1	2	3	4	5
6	7	8	9	10	11	12
13	14	15	16	17	18	19
20	21	22	23	24	25	26
27	28	29	30	31		

April
S	M	T	W	T	F	S
					1	2
3	4	5	6	7	8	9
10	11	12	13	14	15	16
17	18	19	20	21	22	23
24	25	26	27	28	29	30

May
S	M	T	W	T	F	S
1	2	3	4	5	6	7
8	9	10	11	12	13	14
15	16	17	18	19	20	21
22	23	24	25	26	27	28
29	30	31				

June
S	M	T	W	T	F	S
			1	2	3	4
5	6	7	8	9	10	11
12	13	14	15	16	17	18
19	20	21	22	23	24	25
26	27	28	29	30		

July
S	M	T	W	T	F	S
					1	2
3	4	5	6	7	8	9
10	11	12	13	14	15	16
17	18	19	20	21	22	23
24	25	26	27	28	29	30
31						

August
S	M	T	W	T	F	S
	1	2	3	4	5	6
7	8	9	10	11	12	13
14	15	16	17	18	19	20
21	22	23	24	25	26	27
28	29	30	31			

September
S	M	T	W	T	F	S
				1	2	3
4	5	6	7	8	9	10
11	12	13	14	15	16	17
18	19	20	21	22	23	24
25	26	27	28	29	30	

October
S	M	T	W	T	F	S
						1
2	3	4	5	6	7	8
9	10	11	12	13	14	15
16	17	18	19	20	21	22
23	24	25	26	27	28	29
30	31					

November
S	M	T	W	T	F	S
		1	2	3	4	5
6	7	8	9	10	11	12
13	14	15	16	17	18	19
20	21	22	23	24	25	26
27	28	29	30			

December
S	M	T	W	T	F	S
				1	2	3
4	5	6	7	8	9	10
11	12	13	14	15	16	17
18	19	20	21	22	23	24
25	26	27	28	29	30	31

INDEX

PICTURE ACKNOWLEDGEMENTS

The Publishers would like to acknowledge the following companies for the use of illustrations used in this book: Perrier S.A. and The Ariel Press for the reproduction of cartoons from *Some Rules of Golf* by Charles Crombie; The British Golf Museum, St. Andrews and The Royal and Ancient Golf of St. Andrews; I-Contact of Colchester for use of their artwork originally reproduced in the British Golf Museum Souvenir Guide; *Golf Monthly* and Sotheby's.

Notes for Golfers

Notes for Golfers

Notes for Golfers

Notes for Golfers